FIRST
B**O**RN
Second
B**O**RN

# FIRST BORN Second BORN

## Barbara A. Sullivan

CHOSEN BOOKS, Lincoln, Virginia 22078
of The Zondervan Corporation, Grand Rapids, Michigan 49506

Copyright © 1983, Barbara A. Sullivan

Library of Congress Cataloging in Publication:
Sullivan, Barbara A.
  Firstborn, Second-Born
  Bibliography: p.
  1. Birth order.
  2. Christianity—Psychology
I Title.
BF723.B5S89      1983           155.9, 24          83-2011
ISBN 0-310-60381-1

Printed in the United States of America.

Chosen Books is a division of The Zondervan Corporation, Grand Rapids, Michigan 49506. Editorial offices for Chosen Books are in Lincoln, Virginia 22078.

To John, Shannon,
Tom and Kelly who demonstrated
the practical outworkings
of
birth order effects
so perfectly

# Table of Contents

# Acknowledgments

This book would have been impossible without the contribution of my friend and editor, Catherine Jackson. Her patient and meticulous editing and helpful suggestions played a substantial role in the finished product. I owe much to the invaluable research compiled by Dr. Lucille K. Forer in her two books *Birth Order and Life Roles* and *The Birth Order Factor.* It was her work that first piqued my curiosity and subsequently led to the writing of this book. Finally I wish to thank my husband, John, who was willing on more than one occasion to eat hot dogs while I was involved in this project. His constant encouragement and optimism gave me the incentive I needed to finish the manuscript.

# FOREWORD

When I first met Barbara Sullivan, she was just beginning her research into the effects of birth order on one's personality and approach to life. As we became better acquainted, she began pointing out to me that some of my reactions were typically those of an oldest child. I was openly skeptical, pointing out to her that I am *not* a firstborn, since I had an older brother who died before I was born. Her explanation that his early death made me, for all practical purposes, my parents' oldest child left me still unconvinced.

Only when Barbara began sending me her first drafts of the various chapters in this book did I find myself becoming a reluctant convert to her belief that birth order is an important factor in personality development. Her quotations from Alfred Adler, Karl König and other respected authorities in the fields of psychiatry and psychology are impressive, and she makes a good case for her theory that God chose men of a particular birth order to carry out assignments for which their place in the family constellation uniquely qualified them.

Most convincing to me, however, were the reactions of the Christians in her fellowship when she met with the representatives of each birth order to discuss with them her findings relative to their position in the family. In each group, there were many who seemed relieved to know that certain traits they had observed in themselves were characteristics normally associated with their birth order and were shared by others in the group.

Barbara's discussion of biblical characters and her inclusion of comments by real, live, present-day Christians with real, live, present-day problems ensure that this book is no dull rehash of findings from the fields of secular psychology and psychiatry. Whether or not you find in these pages the answer to some of your own problems with self-acceptance, you are sure to find several hours of enjoyable reading and gain a greater understanding of your children, your friends and—more than likely—yourself.

Catherine Jackson

# PREFACE

As leaders of a Christian fellowship composed of some one hundred men and women, my wife, Barbara, and I find that a large part of our ministry is concerned with trying to help each member of the group recognize that he or she is a special creation of God, born for a purpose, blessed with a gift (see I Peter 4:10). Christianity becomes exciting when the believer realizes that he has a role to play and is not intended to be merely a spectator.

Christians in a close-knit fellowship like ours come to think of each other as brothers and sisters. It is not surprising, then, that relationships within the family of God are affected by relationships with the siblings in one's natural family. God has called His children to live together in a spiritual fellowship that surpasses the natural love of brothers and sisters. Often, however, there has been real resistance among the members of our fellowship to the development of close ties within our Christian family.

Barbara and I began searching for an explanation for this resistance, and we discovered that one of the biggest stumblingblocks to the development of close, lasting relationships is an inability to understand and accept ourselves. Peering out from inside ourselves, most of us compare our weaknesses (which we know all too well) with the strengths we see in everyone around us. Our usual conclusion is that other people won't accept us if we allow them to know us as we really are. A few people, on the other hand, see themselves as superior to the rest of their fellow Christians and cast a critical, judgmental eye on those "beneath" them.

In either case, it becomes difficult for us to maintain intimate relationships, and among our friends we are superficial and guarded. The result is fear, loneliness, emotional trauma and, in some cases, mental breakdown—even among God's people.

Barbara has done a good deal of teaching on the various factors affecting our personality and self-image. Birth order is one of the specifics she deals with in her talks to women's groups—and invariably this subject elicits excitement and a desire for more information. Four years ago Barbara began the laborious task of researching and cataloging literature on this subject. She was soon convinced that there is a definite association between birth order and one's approach to life situations. It became obvious that some of the traits people find most difficult to accept, either in themselves or in others, are directly related to their place in the family constellation.

Since all the studies on the subject of birth order have been conducted by secular psychologists and psychiatrists, Barbara saw the need to relate the findings reported there to the growing field of Christian psychology. Therefore, she went to the Bible to study the effects of birth order on the men of God whose lives are portrayed there: Abraham the firstborn, David the youngest, and representatives of all the birth orders between. Her findings intrigued us. In each case, she found that the individual's birth order was one of the factors that qualified him for his use according to God's plan.

After gathering all the information she could from secular and biblical sources, Barbara did some "clinical research" among the members of our fellowship. The representatives of each birth order were invited to meet in our home so that she could share with them her findings about the characteristics associated with their place in the family constellation. Their reactions to these findings, many of which you will read in the following pages, demonstrate clearly that an awareness of the effects of birth order can be an important key to self-understanding and self-acceptance.

Our prayer for you who read this book is that God will use it to give you a better understanding of yourself and of others, and that this understanding may help you to develop a closer relationship with your brothers and sisters—those in your natural family as well as those in the family of God.

Dr. John Sullivan

# Chapter 1

# Relating in God's Family

When my doorbell rang about eight o'clock one Thursday evening, I was delighted to see two young women from our Christian fellowship standing on the doorstep. Patrice and Martha smiled politely as I welcomed them inside, yet I noticed that their faces were clouded.

Without wasting time on small talk, Martha let me know they'd come for more than a social call. "We need to talk to you," she said, with a note of confidentiality.

"Certainly," I replied. "Let's go into the kitchen, and I'll make some coffee."

As I set the coffee brewing, I noticed that my two guests were all but ignoring each other. At once the iciness concerned me, because I knew that these young ladies were close friends. In fact, Patrice was largely responsible for the fact that Martha had committed her life to Jesus four years ago. Since then they had worked closely together, befriending and ministering to other single women, and their complementary personalities made them an effective team.

They had barely settled at the kitchen table when Martha blurted out the reason for their visit.

"Lately Patrice and I are having a real struggle in relating to each other. I'm always reacting angrily to her. I feel she's trying to dominate me."

I glanced at Patrice, who continued to sit quietly with her hands folded. "In what way do you feel dominated, Martha?" I probed, reaching up to get the mugs from the cabinet.

"I can't really put my finger on anything in particular," Martha replied. "And I still love her for all she's done for me. But somehow I just seem to resent any suggestions she makes to me now."

"Patrice, what's your feeling?" I wanted to know.

By this time the three of us were sitting at the kitchen table with mugs of hot coffee. Patrice took a sip before replying thoughtfully. "Chiefly, I guess, I'm puzzled about this break in our relationship. I need to know if I'm doing something I should correct, and I want Martha to find out why she's suddenly begun resenting me."

For the next hour, Martha did most of the talking. I listened to her grievances, and began to get some insight into the problem. The pattern was one with which I was becoming familiar.

Patrice, a firstborn girl, tended to mother the women she led into a new relationship with the Lord. Her protectiveness and the desire to dominate were the normal traits of a firstborn girl, especially one with a younger sister. Martha had responded well to Patrice's mothering until now. What puzzled me was why she was suddenly reacting against it.

Knowing Martha's family background, I turned to her and said, "Could it be that Patrice reminds you of your older sister?" For a moment Martha looked startled, then tears welled up in her eyes. She began to sob openly. Quietly, Patrice and I prayed for the deep healing work of the Holy Spirit that was occurring.

As Martha's weeping subsided, I asked her more questions about her older sister. More pieces of the puzzle fell into place. Martha, the third child and second girl in a family of six, felt that she had been dominated and eclipsed by her aggressive, successful firstborn sister. She didn't enjoy this subordinate position, but she came to feel secure in it. After all, it was the only role she had ever known. When she joined our fellowship, she slid easily into the same dependent position in the family of God. Until recently, she had felt comfortable in this familiar role.

Yes, Martha agreed, there was a parallel between her relationship with her older sister and her friendship with Patrice; but she had no idea why she was rebelling now against her lifelong position of dependency.

As I studied Martha—slim, attractive, feminine—I thought about the transformation the Holy Spirit had effected in the past four years. When Patrice first brought Martha to our fellowship, she was overweight and boyishly dressed. Her somewhat unkempt appearance demonstrated clearly her poor self-image. As Jesus made His love real to her, rebellion and inferiority feelings gradually gave way to acceptance of responsibility, self-acceptance, confidence and poise. The inner change was soon reflected in her physical appearance, and the Martha who sat in my kitchen now was a beautiful woman, engaged to a young man in our fellowship.

Suddenly the answer grew clear. Martha was finally rejecting the subordinate role she had always assumed. She was now secure enough in Jesus' love and in the family of God to be set free from the bondage brought about by her childhood position in her own family.

I shared this growing realization with Patrice and Martha— and the response was overwhelming. The iciness was gone, and the warming love of God flowed once again between these estranged friends. Then Patrice prayed that God would cut the spiritual umbilical cord that had bound Martha to her, and asked the Holy Spirit to bring forth in Martha the gifts and ministries He had given her.

When they left my home that night, Patrice and Martha

were no longer teacher and disciple, but friends and coequals in the Kingdom of God. Martha is now leading a girls' Bible study group—something she could never have done if she had remained in her dependent position. God had allowed her to retain this accustomed position for a time after she came into His family, but it was never His intention to let her remain forever handicapped by the negative effects of her birth order. Once she had been crippled by her past, retarded in her spiritual maturity. Now she is free.

The Christian community needs to understand the effects of birth order on one's life and personality. The visit from Martha and Patrice gave me the incentive to dig deeper into the subject. In my own life, and in the lives of Christian brothers and sisters, I saw the effects of our childhood "positions" helping or hampering our growth as men and women in the Body of Christ.

The springboard for my research came from some of the greatest psychologists of our time.

Alfred Adler, the Austrian psychiatrist, is usually credited with being the first to recognize the effects of birth order on human personality and, indeed, the whole structure of society:

> The position in the family leaves an indelible stamp upon the style of life. Every difficulty of development is caused by rivalry and lack of cooperation in the family. If we look around at our social life and ask why rivalry and competition is its most obvious aspect— indeed, not only at our social life but at our whole world—then we must recognize that people are everywhere pursuing the goal of being conqueror, of overcoming and surpassing others. This goal is the result of training in early child-

hood, of the rivalries and competitive striving of children who have not felt themselves an equal part of their whole family.[1]

Adler's original research on birth order effects has been followed by more than a thousand revealing studies on the subject. Why are these discoveries of concern to the Christian? Because placement in our natural family can make an indelible stamp on our relationships within the family of God. Writes psychologist Karl König,

> The family-constellation . . . shapes the *social* behaviour of man. It determines the way he reacts to other people, how he is able to make friends or not, the way he finds companionship and community with others. Even the choice of a husband or wife is deeply influenced by the facts of the family-constellation.[2]

The Christian who grew up in a home where there was serious sibling rivalry may find it difficult to enter into close relationships within his church family. Says Elizabeth Hurlock, a well-known educator at the University of Chicago:

> The serious aspect of sibling friction is that it becomes a pattern of social relationships which the child is likely to carry outside the home and apply to his relationships with the peer group. . . . Also, sibling friction weakens the child's motivation to form social relationships with people outside the home. When his relationships with his siblings are not pleasant, he has little motivation to expand his social contacts further.[3]

God calls His people into a family-type relationship under His fatherhood. And today churches are experimenting with communal living and with "cluster families"—diverse groups of families and individuals who meet together on a regular basis, with the goal of learning to care for one another as they care for members of their own nuclear family. In the family of God, Christians are beginning to experience a fulfillment of Jesus' promise: "And every one who has left houses or brothers or sisters or father or mother or children or lands for My name's sake will receive a hundredfold . . . " (Matthew 19:29, The New King James Bible).

In a close-knit Christian fellowship we find *many* sisters and brothers, and sometimes mothers, fathers and children. So it is not surprising that people who have had unhappy relationships with members of their own childhood families often find conflict and strain where there ought to be peace—in God's family.

As our own Christian fellowship began to draw closer together, problems arose among various members of the group. Soon it became clear to my husband and me that most of these problems were the result of unresolved childhood conflicts with siblings and parents. Even the born-again Christians who make up our spiritual family brought with them the strife, envy and jealousy they had grown up with in their natural families.

Think about your own friendships and associations with other Christians. Do you ever wonder why you feel drawn to some members of your church or prayer group and almost repelled by others? Could it be that these new brothers and sisters in God's family are identified, on the subconscious level, with a favorite sister in your childhood family, or perhaps with a brother who was an intense rival? Or are you an only child? Never having had brothers and sisters, do you find it hard to share God's love—and perhaps the attention of your pastor or group leader—with so many brothers and sisters in Christ?

As I continued my reading in this field, I became aware that my birth order affects not only my relationships within the family of God, but also my attitude toward my husband and children. Lucille Forer, author and clinical psychologist, asks these pertinent questions:

> Are you, as oldest child, in conflict with your own oldest child because both you and he would like to be in charge of situations and tell the others what to do? As youngest child are you perhaps a bit competitive with your own youngest child for any indulgences that might be available? [4]

I myself am second to a brilliant older brother, and I have a very gifted firstborn son. One day it struck me that too often I was taking the side of my second-born daughter against her older brother. I had to face the fact that I was still fighting childhood battles—trying to make up for the frustration I had felt in my efforts to compete with my brother. When I understood why I tended to overprotect my second child at the expense of the eldest, I was able to become a fairer and better arbiter of my children's disagreements.

Similarly, my firstborn friend Betty has no difficulty in relating to the daughter who shares her birth order. Her problem is with her second daughter, Nancy. We were discussing this problem one day when the realization struck Betty that her irritation with Nancy is greatest when she and her husband (also a second-born) are having difficulties. She was transferring negative emotions from one to the other because her husband and her second-born daughter are so similar in temperament. With this insight Betty's attitude changed, and she was able to show more love and acceptance toward Nancy.

When Jesus said, "This is my commandment, That ye love one another, as I have loved you" (John 15:12, KJV), He meant what He said. Those of us who are serious about following this command need all the help we can get—and this includes help from the fields of psychology and psychiatry and help from God's Word. If I naturally bring into my marriage and into my spiritual family the role I have learned in my childhood family, I need to understand *why* I act or react in ways that make me hard to live with and hard to love.

I have learned that each birth order is associated with certain strengths and weaknesses that affect our growth as Christians. Recognizing our tendency to these characteristics does not mean that we consider them fixed or irreversible traits. Rather, we can seek the help of the Holy Spirit in utilizing our strengths and overcoming our weaknesses. Unless we recognize those weaknesses, we are not likely to ask for His help in dealing with them.

Birth order, of course, is only one of myriad factors that make us the unique individuals we are. This particular factor, however, has an unusually direct impact on our relationships. And in recognizing the influence of birth order on our families, natural and spiritual, we can start to free ourselves and our children from traits that would stunt spiritual and emotional growth. We can take a major step toward allowing God to perfect His strength in our weakness (II Corinthians 12:9).

# Chapter 2

# The Family "Constellation"

"Why can't you be more responsible, like your sister?"

"Your brother would never do such a foolish thing!"

"My oldest child is the one with the brains. The younger one—well, I guess he'll be an athlete."

How many of us still wince when we recall criticisms like these that were directed at us as children? How many times have we as adults made such devastating comparisons about our own children? In too many homes today, one or both parents use criticism and negative comparisons and hope to get positive results with their children!

At the root of it, parents often fail to recognize that each of their children is an individual—a unique creation of almighty God—and that there is no justification for comparing them.

Let's look at it from the viewpoint of the newborn. Each child must find a compatible place among parents, brothers and sisters who have already established their "orbit" in the family constellation. In an environment charged with many, many variables—hopes, expectations, demands and comparisons—comes the newborn. As adults, we can help to build a healthy self-image in that child by first understanding some of the crucial factors that shape him, even before birth!

One variable in the climate surrounding each child is the

parents' emotional response to his arrival. The feeling of excitement and anticipation, mixed with tension and anxiety, that is associated with the birth of the first child diminishes with each successive pregnancy. Most mothers become more relaxed and self-assured with the advent of each child. Occasionally a mother even has to fight outright resentment when she learns that she is pregnant *again!*

Even the physiological conditions affecting the developing fetus and its birth may be different for each child. As Lucille Forer says:

> It is possible that birth order may have some effect on the individual's development even as he is still unborn. Some authorities believe that each pregnancy of the mother may change the intrauterine conditions for each following child.
>
> Birth conditions may themselves be affected by the birth order of the child coming into the world. The duration of labor has been reported as much as fifty percent higher for first born children, and the point has been made that they may therefore be subject to a higher degree of cerebral compression.
>
> It is therefore possible that some of the differences we find between first born and later born children may be the result of varying physical conditions of the mother and problems besetting first pregnancies and labor. [1]

Too, the genetic inheritance from the parents may change from child to child:

> There are indications that as a person grows older, changes may occur in individual germ cells. Physical

or chemical forces, such as nuclear radiation and drugs, may alter the machinery of cell development. Therefore, the germ cells which create a later child may be different from those that existed when an earlier child was conceived. [2]

Another factor that varies with each child, of course, is the parents' influence on his personality. We will look into this in greater depth in subsequent chapters, but generally speaking, certain patterns have emerged. It is the firstborn who bears the brunt of the parents' expectations and discipline. The second-born is influenced not only by the parents (whose attention and discipline are now divided), but by the child ahead of him as well. In a larger family, in fact, younger children may be influenced more by their siblings than by their parents.

But determining one's place in the family constellation is not as simple as it might seem. It is not just a matter of counting the number of children born ahead of you. Age and sex differences, family size, parental influence, adoption, twins, the disability or death of an older sibling—all are factors that modify the effects of birth order.

"The smaller the age gap between siblings," says Walter Toman, a German professor of psychology, "the more severe their conflicts with each other, but the greater also their inclination not to let go of each other in later life."[3] Siblings who are six or more years apart, on the other hand, tend to grow up more like single children, he says. Therefore, an individual whose brothers and sisters are all much older or younger than he will probably show many characteristics of an only child.

Toman also believes that the effects of sex differences between siblings are tied in with those of age differences. They have a direct bearing on the degree of competition between siblings, and on the influence of one child upon another.

To begin with, a child under the age of four, regardless of sex, will generally see a new baby as a rival, a threat to his power and position. As the relationship develops, however, both children may grow to feel more secure in their position. The most comfortable relationship seems to develop between a firstborn boy with a younger sister. A child who is the only one of his or her sex among siblings is in a favorable position and tends to have high self-esteem.

A family of all boys or all girls increases the birth order effects on all the children. For instance, all the leadership qualities of the firstborn are accentuated in the oldest brother of brothers.

A mixture of sexes among siblings seems to soften the effects of birth order. Lucille Forer believes that

> sisters with brothers seem more influenced toward adoption of opposite-sex characteristics than are brothers with sisters. If brothers have sisters close in age, their own male characteristics may be intensified, while the sisters often adopt male interests and attitudes. This may occur in the girls because male attributes still seem more prestigious in our society.[4]

Karl König believes that there are only three personality types in all families, no matter how many children the family contains. He says:

> The firstborn attempts to conquer the world.
> The second-born tries to live in harmony with the world.

*The third-born* is inclined to escape the direct meeting with the world.[5]

He also notes an intriguing pattern emerging after those
first three children: that the fourth, fifth and sixth child follow
the characteristics of the first, second and third, as do the
seventh, eighth and ninth; and so on.

James Bossard holds a different point of view. In an original
study of 100 large families with six or more children, he found
different personality patterns emerging in the later-born siblings:

The first ones to appear develop patterns of responsibility because they are first and are followed
by younger and more helpless siblings. The next
ones, finding this role pre-empted, seek recognition
. . . with their personal charms. The next children,
finding these two roles pre-empted, turn from the
family to the community. They become social-mind-
ed and socially ambitious. Those that follow in turn
have to turn to a new avenue of achievement. . . .
They become the scholars. . . . Finding all of these
avenues under active cultivation, the next child withdraws from competition. . . . Or he may not withdraw his presence, only his sense of responsibility. . . . Finally, at the end of the line is the terminal
child, either pampered into relative ineffectiveness
or wearing the "magic boots" to overtake the older
ones.[6]

Children who grow up in large families, Bossard points out,
agree that such an upbringing socializes them considerably.
Their play and work together promotes interdependence and
helps them to learn to live together.

When have Christians needed to learn about living together more than today, in our age of independence? The apostle Paul often warns those of us in the family of God not to be independent but interdependent. Our society trains us to be like the foot that says, "Because I am not a hand, I do not belong to the body" (I Corinthians 12:15, NIV), or the eye that says to the hand, "I don't need you" (verse 21.) The independent spirits among us seem to come much more often from small families rather than larger ones. Somehow God intends to fit all of us—regardless of our family backgrounds or personality traits—into a smoothly functioning, supportive Body of Christ.

How do we smooth our rough edges, overcoming personal traits that we dislike? How do we learn to love one another as Christ commanded, making the family of God a caring, nurturing shelter that will attract others? Certainly a major step is discovering those early influences that continue to work in our lives, sometimes forcing us apart from others.

Some of the variables that affect a child's character development are harder to trace. Yet researchers have found that the effects of birth order are intensified in the child whose place in the family constellation is the same as one or both of his parents. Lucille Forer notes, interestingly, that the influence is greatest upon firstborn children and increases with each generation.

> Often this second generation oldest child becomes excessively rebellious, tense, and angry. The possibility that this might occur increases when the first child is a third or fourth generation first child. He receives the full impact of rigid consciences and disciplinary attitudes. In such cases it is very impor-

tant for parents to develop tolerance and gentleness in their relations with their child.[7]

A child who is adopted as a baby will show the characteristics associated with his place in his *adoptive* family. If anything, being adopted tends to increase the natural drive of the oldest child in a family to achieve competence and approval. Dr. Forer believes this is because:

> Adoptive parents may feel somewhat "on stage" as parents. They may believe they are being watched by the agency which placed the child with them, as well as by neighbors and relatives challenging them to demonstrate their prowess as parents. Thus, they may be more tense and anxious than they would be otherwise, and communicate some of this anxiety to their child, especially the first child. If they adopt others, they are likely to be more sure of themselves with later children.[8]

Brian was adopted as an infant, the first child in his adoptive family. He was an exceptionally tense and striving man when he joined our fellowship after years of judicious scrutiny and correction and competition against a high standard.

The child who is adopted after infancy will bring at least some of the role he learned from his former surroundings into his new adoptive family. In many cases, however, these characteristics can be outweighed by the effects of his place in this new adoptive family constellation.

Unbelievable as it sounds, even twins seem to be affected by their order of birth. With them, the order of delivery tends to have the same effect on personality as the birth order of single children.

In a study reported in 1969, the personality traits of each child in 24 sets of twins (ten identical and fourteen fraternal) were studied by their mothers and also by experimenters.[9] On the basis of the descriptions given from a checklist of adjectives, and after observing the twins for a period of time, the experimenters made an educated guess as to the birth order of each child. If the twins were the first children born to the mother, the older would be the firstborn child; the younger, the second-born. If the mother already had one child, the twins were second- and third-born children.

The adjectives that led the experimenters to place a child in one of the three birth orders were the following:

> *Firstborn:*     adult-oriented, leader, responsible, mature for age, ambitious, aggressive
>
> *Second-born:*   easygoing, cheerful, stubborn, light-hearted, unconcerned, gentle
>
> *Third-born:*    self-conscious, immature for age, withdrawn, very emotional, quiet, distrustful

In all but two cases, the guesses were correct. (The odds that such a high percentage of correct guesses would occur by chance are 50,000:1.) In one of these two cases, the twins had been delivered by Caesarean section, making it impossible to determine their natural birth order. In the other case, the twins followed an older sibling who was the victim of a crippling disease; both of these twins had personality traits of a firstborn.

Charlie, a young man in our fellowship, is a twin. His sister, born only minutes ahead of him, retained the leadership throughout their childhood. She was aggressive and outgoing while Charlie was quiet and submissive. To this day, Charlie reacts negatively to aggressive, domineering women—evidence that he still resents, subconsciously, his sister's rule over him.

After talking with Charlie, I was curious to see if the Bible listed any specific traits in describing its most famous twins, Esau and Jacob. Turning to Genesis 25, where their story begins, I was amazed to learn that these men did indeed display characteristics of first- and second-born sons. Esau, the first out of the womb, was aggressive by nature, "a skillful hunter, a man of the open country," while Jacob is described as "a quiet man, staying among the tents" (Genesis 25:27, NIV). Here was one account among many in the Bible in which the effects of birth order was strongly evident.

If some physical or mental defect makes it impossible for one child to assume his role in the family, the effects of birth order take an interesting turn. The child next in line will usually show the characteristics normally associated with the preceding child's birth order, rather than his own.

One family in our fellowship had a brain-damaged firstborn son who remained a helpless infant throughout his nine years of life. His sister, one year younger, took on the role of a firstborn, assuming responsibilities far beyond her years. The third child, a boy, has the personality traits of a second-born.

Like severe retardation or physical disability, the early death of an older sibling tends to move the next child one rung higher on the ladder of birth order effects. I have seen this demonstrated in my own family. Although my Uncle Adam was the fifth child of seven, he had many of the characteristics of a firstborn. The firstborn girl was almost eight when he was born, and the three intervening children died before his birth. These deaths, together with the wide age difference between him and his sister, have made him understandably more like a firstborn than a fifth-born.

In the event of physical disability or death, it is natural for other children to take on the role of older siblings. And yet there are emotional and spiritual disabilities that can cripple a child and damage his self-image. Some children are so wounded by events beyond their control that they see themselves as having little or no value. They may retreat from the inborn, natural role prescribed by their birth order, and come to feel that they are not even a part of their own family.

This kind of unfortunate situation developed in the family of a young man I met recently.

Peter, a bright, charming man, told me that his parents had been more or less forced to marry young because his mother had gotten pregnant. Shortly after their marriage, Peter's older brother was born, and grew up during a very turbulent time in his parents' relationship. Since he was the innocent "cause" of their forced match, he bore the brunt of all their anger and hostility. Such bitter arguments are most often translated by children as rejection.

Two years later, when the parents were on better terms, Peter was born. The past was somewhat forgiven and forgotten with the coming of a legitimate child. Three other children arrived in the coming years. But the effects on the oldest son were already set.

Far from remembering his brother as a leader or hero-figure, Peter says, "I really don't remember much about him as we were growing up. He was there, of course, but always in the background. He was always like a shadow, a nonentity in our house."

In a very real way, Peter's older brother *was* a shadow, a constant reminder of his parents' sin and shame and hard times. They did not play up his arrival in the world, as new parents normally do, and through the early years of his life, they all but ignored his very existence in an attempt to forget their troubled situation.

Small wonder the boy was quiet, oversensitive and unaggressive. Later, he did poorly in school, struggling to keep up with other children intellectually and physically. Rarely did he find a close friend.

Peter, on the other hand, very naturally assumed the role of the firstborn without the pressures that usually rest on a child in that position. He got the best of both birth order positions— the calm, agreeable nature of a second child along with the drive, gifts and leadership abilities of the first. His two younger brothers and his younger sister all looked to him as their role model—a position that is also normally enjoyed by the first child. "Even today," Peter says, "I'm the one they call on if there's a problem in the family."

As Peter's family demonstrates, our position in the family constellation may be less important in determining our "birth order" than the way we view that position. While our placement in the family has a definite effect on our personalities, it is our response to this placement—whether we accept or reject the role we are given in our childhood home—that has the greater influence.

Personally, I was the second child in our family, and I always disliked being "second-best." After I became a Christian, I slowly recognized that God had planned the order of my birth as well as every other aspect of my life, and I was able to thank Him for giving me my particular place in the family. I could see that He had used my birth order—and all the varied factors that built my personality—to ready me for my place in His scheme of things.

It is my hope that this book will enable other Christians to accept their place in the family constellation and, with the help of the Holy Spirit, to make the most of the strengths and weaknesses associated with their birth order.

# Chapter 3

## The Firstborn

After the plane was airborne, I pushed the button on the arm of my seat and eased myself back into a comfortable position. My husband and I were returning home after a long-awaited vacation, and I wanted to savor my last hours of freedom from responsibility.

Eavesdropping wasn't my intention, but I couldn't help hearing the conversation behind me. A middle-aged woman was telling her seatmate, a young man in his twenties, about her two grown daughters.

"I just don't understand my younger daughter," she said. "No matter what her older sister says or does, she resents it."

"I think I understand why she's resentful," the young man replied. "I'm the oldest of three children and was always the role model for the others, whether I wanted to be or not. My parents and teachers always used me as the standard to judge my younger brother and sister by. I was a real achiever, and the others never quite lived up to my performance level—especially as my folks saw it. As a result, my brother and sister grew up resenting me. Now they make a practice of criticizing everything I say, do and think."

What a coincidence that I should tune in on their conversation! Only weeks before, I had come across an engrossing,

thoroughly helpful book called *The Eldest Child* by Dr. Edith
Neisser. The young man behind me was echoing the author's
statement that

> later children are inevitably looked upon as "faster"
> or "slower," "even cuter" or "less good looking" than
> the first one. No matter how earnestly mothers and
> fathers promise themselves not to make compari-
> sons, the first child has set a pattern.[1]

Just a few days before leaving on our vacation, my husband
and I had met with the firstborns in our fellowship and asked
them to discuss their feelings about being the oldest child in
the family. We found that the position of "standard-bearer"
was not so privileged or comfortable as it might sound.

In my mind now I could see Linda—hands gesticulating,
blonde hair bobbing—as she told about her childhood home,
where she was the oldest of four girls.

"I was supposed to be the example for my sisters," she said.
"My parents' favorite remark was, 'We expect such behavior
from the younger girls but not from you, Linda.' I always felt
that I was on display. Maybe this is why I developed such a
strict conscience and became so conforming."

Linda's remarks, and those of the young airplane pas-
senger, underscore the unique privileges and pressures of
being a firstborn. In no other child does birth order have so
great an effect in shaping character. In fact, throughout the
ages, firstborns have stood on an unusual pedestal built of
myth, spirituality and tradition.

Several studies delve into the folklore and even superstition
surrounding oldest children. In one of these studies, Dr.
Neisser says:

> Among the Ugandans in East Africa, if the first child

was a boy, he was promptly killed. They believed he would take his father's strength, absorb his father's spirit, and bring about his end. Entering into this twisted thinking was also the idea that the father was born again in his first son. Both could not survive.[2]

On the same subject, Dr. König writes,

> In primal times, the first born child did not even belong to the parents. It was considered to be the property of the divine being who was the leader of the tribe or clan or people. Most of the first born children were sacrificed either at the ancient altars, or by exposure to the elements.[3]

Among the Jews in Old Testament times, however, the place and destiny of firstborns was strikingly different. My search through Scripture, with the help of a Bible dictionary, showed me that even during the time of Christ, every first-born male, human or animal, was called "holy to the Lord" (Luke 2:23, KJV). The first male child was redeemed at the temple by a special sacrifice, and from then on enjoyed a privileged position. He received his father's chief blessing, in the tradition of the patriarchs; his portion of the inheritance was twice that of any of his brothers (in accordance with Jewish law as set down in Deuteronomy 21:17); he became the priest in his household; and, after his father's death, he became the patriarch of the family.[4]

At first I was puzzled. Acts 10:34 tells us that God shows no partiality, yet He seemed to me extraordinarily partial to first-born sons. Though His ways are sovereign, and many times inscrutable, I found an enlightening clue in a quotation from Lucille Forer:

The first born child has often been described as
representing the "past" of society, as compared with
the later born child who is described as being concerned with the practical aspects of present society.
It is claimed that the first child tends to carry the past
into the present because he adheres to the standards
of his parents and these standards come from the
past.[5]

Studies have indeed shown that the first child tends to be
the most conservative—the defender of faith and tradition,
the maintainer of the status quo. So the Creator, knowing that
the oldest child would be the one most likely to have this
tendency, directed that the lion's share of the inheritance—
spiritual, material and cultural—should go to the firstborn
son. He was a link with the past, the one most likely to see that
God's ordinances amd family traditions were passed on from
generation to generation.

There is, of course, another side to this view of firstborns.
As Karl König points out, there are

two characteristics of a first child. He can either bar
the way or bridge the past and the future. He has two
faces—one is turned to his parents who represent
the past; the other looks on to his brothers and
sisters, thereby gazing into the future. The position
of the first child has a most important function in the
whole flow of the river of life.[6]

Perhaps it is because the firstborn tends to be somewhat
rigid and inflexible that God used a *younger* son when He
wanted to do something new. Jacob, who fathered the twelve
tribes of Israel, was a second-born son. David, the king whom

God selected to be a prototype of the Messiah, was the youngest of eight boys.

Since the firstborn son was regarded by the Jews as an extension of the father, a curse on this son was one of the strongest that could be given. When Pharaoh persisted in opposing God's command to "let my people go," he was finally punished by the death of his own firstborn son and "all the firstborn in the land of Egypt, both man and beast" (Exodus 12:12, KJV). Since the oldest child is the first issue of the father's strength—the one who will usually be most like his father—cutting off the firstborn son ensured that the father's character would not be completely reproduced in the next generation.

Unlike the younger children, who have their older siblings as role models, the oldest child has only his parents as a model. Hence, he tends to emulate their behavior more closely than do his brothers or sisters. His prolonged association with adults also has the effect of making him more serious than the other children.

When parents have difficulty with their first child, it is usually in those areas where their own weaknesses lie. Dr. Forer says that the first born is especially apt to copy

> the behavior and attitudes which [the parents] displayed in directing and disciplining him, their ways of being parental. Thus he is kind and tolerant or stern and disciplining in relating to other people, and particularly to his own dependents, just as his parents were in reacting to him. His feelings about himself and what he expects of himself will depend, too, upon his parents' attitude and expectations directed toward him.[7]

So the full impact of the parents' discipline and standards are brought to bear on the first child. Instead of letting him develop at his own pace, Mother will do everything in her power to see that he sits, stands, walks, talks and is potty-trained at the proper age. This push for achievement becomes a way of life for the firstborn; he is likely to be more achievement-oriented and less people-oriented than later children.

In my own family, I discovered that I was disciplining my oldest child most frequently, although he really needs it the least. I was generally more lenient with my youngest child, even though she needs the greatest amount of discipline. My oldest child is also the one from whom I expect the most, and he still bears the brunt of my push for achievement.

The oldest child tends to incorporate the values of his parents into his own conscience, so that he goes through life with a strong "parent within." The oldest child may develop an oversensitized conscience, and parents need to guard against the danger of creating a guilt complex in their firstborn. Too often, parents manipulate such children by making them feel guilty, or by playing on their desire to win approval.

In Chapter 1, I mentioned Patrice, who is one of the first-borns in our fellowship. Before she was a Christian, Patrice was tormented by a demanding, oversensitive conscience that gave her no rest, day or night. When she heard the gospel— that a forgiving God had already paid the price for every sin she could ever commit—she knew that this was what she needed. Jesus Christ freed Patrice from an overburdening conscience; and John and I have found that this is often the most effective key to unlock the inner struggles of a firstborn.

## Dethronement

Alfred Adler coined the term "dethroned child" to describe the firstborn after the birth of a younger sibling. The phrase is an apt one, since it suggests that the firstborn is indeed "King Baby" until the day another baby arrives and shoves him off the throne.

If you are a parent, perhaps you can remember the mixture of joy and anxiety with which you awaited the birth of your first child. You and your spouse probably spent hours thinking of names for boys and girls, decorating and furnishing the nursery, and imagining what it would be like to have your marriage become a threesome. You absorbed all sorts of ideas, positive and negative, concerning the care and feeding of children—and you were determined to "do right" by your first offspring.

When the great event finally took place, all the anxiety, love, care, attention and discipline that two people could muster were focused on this tiny newcomer. Time after time he was checked against the latest "baby book" (in my day it was Dr. Spock) to see if he was developing "normally." A pictorial record of his progress was preserved in the family album— which in most cases contains five times as many snapshots of the firstborn as of *all* succeeding children. All this attention convinces the firstborn that he is truly the center of the world.

Then one day, Mother goes to the hospital and comes home with another baby, who now has first place in her arms and who gets the greater share of her time and attention. Jealousy is soon simmering inside the firstborn. According to Dr. Forer,

> what occurs first in the reactions of the first child is bewilderment and a feeling of having been abandoned. Jealousy is a later development and seems to appear after the child discovers the full extent of the other child's participation in receiving affection, attention and gifts from the parents.[8]

What happens to the first child when he realizes he has a

rival? He becomes a defender, striving to defend his established position, to regain his conquered place. In many cases he fights for his mother's love—sometimes by being naughty, sometimes by physically attacking the second child, and sometimes by resorting to babyish behavior like soiling his pants or demanding his milk in a bottle instead of a cup or glass. If Mother fights back at him, says Alfred Adler, the child may become

> high-tempered, wild, critical and disobedient. When he turns against his mother, it often happens that his father gives him a chance to renew the old favorable position. He becomes interested in his father and tries to win his attention and affection. Oldest children frequently prefer their fathers and lean toward their side. . . . If a child prefers his father, we know that he has previously suffered a tragedy; he has felt slighted and left out of account; he cannot forget it and his whole style of life is built around this feeling.[9]

In most cases, however, the child turns to other tactics when he finds that babyish behavior will not reestablish his former reign. He may become a conformist and a "people-pleaser." As Lucille Forer says,

> He tries to conform to the parents' standards. He tries to cope with the responsibilities. He tries to be like his parents. The attitude and behavior that offer the best chance of success in pleasing his parents are those which the parents themselves display. So the older child begins a process of being "parental" in relationships with other people.[10]

In some extreme cases, a child's sense of rejection is acute. If the parents do not help with the adjustment, serious problems can erupt—even in adulthood.

This is what happened to a young woman, whom I will call Marie, when her younger brother was born. Feeling rejected by her mother, she turned to her father, who also rejected her. Consequently, Marie grew up rebellious and resentful, with a hatred for all forms of authority. She now exhibits a manic-depressive behavior pattern that is only partially controlled by lithium.

Marie's rebellious and resentful attitude, which is more typical of firstborn boys than of firstborn girls, is doubtless attributable to the double rejection she experienced. According to Forer,

> the older daughter usually does not become defiant and rebellious, and so she maintains the support of the parents. Instead of acting out the tensions she feels about retaining the love of her parents as the older boy might, she tends to turn the tension within and to suffer physical ills. In adult life she often has migraine headaches, and some instances of alcoholic or drug addiction in the older of two sisters have seemed to result from tension caused by wishes to achieve according to the parents' standards.[11]

When the two oldest children are boys, intense competition may result. Dr. Forer believes that the "boy-boy family" produces more serious behavior problems than any other sibling combination. In most cases the younger brother seems to suffer most from this competition, which stimulates achievement in the older boy. Walter Toman says,

> The oldest brother of brothers loves to lead and
> assume responsibility for other persons, particularly
> for men. He tries to take care of them and sometimes
> even to boss them around. He worries more about
> the future than others do. He may derive his claim
> for leadership from these worries.[12]

As I mentioned in Chapter 2, the most comfortable position
in the two-child family seems to be that of the firstborn son
who is followed by a girl. The boy's desire to retain his status
as the oldest child may cause him to accentuate his masculinity. Even though his mother usually continues to give
him special attention because he is the "preferred sex," he
moves naturally to identification with his father. When he
marries, points out Lucille Forer, the older brother of a sister
often expects his wife to wait on him hand and foot, himself
unwilling to assume "feminine" tasks.[13]

An article by Richard D. Lyons in the February 8, 1979,
*Chicago Tribune* revealed that the pages of *Who's Who* seem to be
dominated by only children and firstborn sons. One reason
may be that these two groups, because of their conservative
nature and desire to achieve, tend to choose professions for
their life's work. Another possible explanation is that the
oldest child is, in the majority of families, the most advan-
taged.

The exceptions are seen in large families in which the older
children are often exploited, intentionally or unintentionally,
by their parents. In a study of 100 families with six or more
children, Dr. James Bossard found that in many cases,

> One or two of the older children were called upon to
> carry a large part of the responsibility of rearing the

younger ones, and did so at a sacrifice, often considerable, of their own interests and desires.[14]

In many large families, and in broken homes, the firstborn
may be called upon to act as surrogate mother or father.
Placing such a responsibility on the oldest child may reinforce
his identification with his parent(s) and widen the gap between him and his siblings.

In our fellowship there are two men who were the firstborns
in large families. Bill was the oldest of six children. After his
parents were divorced, his father was given custody of the
children. Since he was busy with his job, he gave Bill charge of
the others. Immediately a gap opened. As Bill describes the
situation, "There was them—the younger children—and then
there was me." Already insecure because of his parents' divorce, Bill was made even more insecure by being put into a
role he had not asked for and was not prepared to accept.

Ron, the oldest of nine children, says he felt "exploited." His
parents could not make ends meet, and Ron was unable to
fulfill his dream of becoming a pilot in the Air Force because he
had to drop out of school and go to work to help out financial-
ly.

With these factors in mind, we can see why a firstborn often
feels ill-at-ease with his peer group, especially if he is from a
large family. Being a helper to his parents and a parent-
surrogate to his siblings, he is neither fish nor fowl. All his
family relationships are with either those in authority over
him or those who are under his authority. At home, he has no
peers.

How will the unique characteristics of the firstborn affect his
or her spiritual life and relationships within the family of God?
Meeting with a sample group of firstborns to discuss this and

other questions, my husband and I discovered some remarkable insights, which I'll share in the next chapter.

# Chapter 4

# Free to Be Me

Seated comfortably around our family room were many of our firstborn friends, whom we'd invited to be part of a sample group, comparing experiences as oldest children. The talk was mostly light and casual—until Susan spoke up:

"You know, I never felt that I had a personality of my own."

Immediately all eyes were riveted on her, and the room seemed charged with anticipation. Not long before, Susan and her husband, Bob, had come to John and me seeking help in overcoming some bitter resentments. Now I sensed that she was about to turn an important key and open the way for a heart-to-heart discussion. As she continued, the room was still.

"After I was born again, my strongest desire was just to be *real*. My parents had trained me to be phony by insisting that I always act pleasant and cheerful, no matter how I was feeling. As a result, I let a lot of anger build up inside me for years."

Susan then told us about her early Christian experiences. "The church Bob and I attended seemed to set a definite pattern for what a Christian woman should be like. I threw myself into church work, doing all the things I thought were expected of me. The more I tried to fit the pattern, the phonier I felt. I equated God with the church, and so I was angry with

Him. I didn't have a 'burden for lost souls' like everyone else, and I felt terribly guilty."

The problem grew so bad that she eventually refused to go to church with Bob at all. It was at this point that they came to talk with John and me. I recalled my first impressions of them—faces lined with concern and deep frustration.

Through our talk that day, we got to know Susan as a very practical person. But because of that practicality, she felt she wasn't spiritual according to her false image of "the godly woman." Bob, an idealist and dreamer, always sought a scriptural injunction to guide him in every situation, while Susan dealt with the practical outworkings of a problem as she could foresee it. Bob's "spiritual" attitude left her feeling guilty.

At one point, Susan had blurted out, "I guess I'm just a backslider."

Gently John had replied, "You're not backslidden; you're just being yourself."

Facing the group in our family room now, Susan's face was lit with a peaceful smile. "Those were the most liberating words I'd ever heard. They helped me to see that there is no set pattern for a child of God. I was suddenly free to be myself and let God develop all my abilities and talents in His way."

Susan's story opened the way for candor in the meeting, and a flood of similar stories followed. Several others in the room told about their struggles to model themselves after a person or group that, to them, exemplified Christianity. Again and again, we heard about their "need to conform."

As we noted in the previous chapter, a firstborn often battles to live up to a certain standard, usually hoping to gain his parents' approval. It may, in fact, become a lifelong problem for the child. Growing up with no real sense of identity, he tends to take on the personality and imitate the mannerisms of people he admires.

Brian, an articulate and successful salesman, then told us about a serious situation that grew out of his tendency to imitate. It sounded frighteningly reminiscent of *The Three Faces of Eve.*

"Most of my selling is done by telephone," Brian told us. "And I developed a high-powered, three-person partnership—only I was all three partners.

"First, I'd call a prospective client as the 'sales manager,' then as 'vice-president.' Finally, I'd call as the 'administrative vice-president.' With each new title, I assumed a different name, voice and personality. I got to be very good at switching roles. Too good, in fact."

One day, Brian explained, he came to the disturbing realization that, in his successful identification with his fictitious personalities, *he was actually losing his own identity.* Then came the conviction that he had been practicing deception. He immediately confessed his sin and asked forgiveness from God. For a while, he told us, he had to battle to keep from reverting to those three personalities.

After Brian's unusual story, Ron pursued the subject of conformity down a different trail. Smiling sheepishly, he admitted, "I conform outwardly to people's expectations, but inside I feel that my way is best and that someday people will recognize this. Are other firstborns like me?"

The others were laughing and nodding assent. Susan answered for the rest of the group: "I always felt I could do anything and do it better than anybody else."

I sensed that the discussion was headed in a crucial direction, so I posed the question: "As firstborns, then, would you say that the most subtle snare for the oldest child is the tendency to conform outwardly while rebelling inwardly?"

Almost before I'd finished, everyone was nodding vigorously. And as we probed further, we decided that the constant prayer of the firstborn should be, "Father, make me *real.* Knit together my inner feelings with my outward expressions."

John and I have found in our study, and through our association with firstborns, that because of inward rebellion, the oldest child often finds that he will not submit to the leadership of anyone in his peer group—that is, someone whom he sees as an equal, a "brother" rather than a "parent."

In the Bible, Abram (before he became Abraham) is a good example of outward conformity that masks inward rebellion. The firstborn son of Terah, he was the oldest of three boys. After Terah's death, God told Abram to leave all his kindred and lands and go to the place where He would direct him. "So Abram went, as the Lord had told him; *and Lot went with him*" (Genesis 12:4, RSV; italics added). As the firstborn, Abram felt a natural responsibility for the welfare of his nephew Lot. In this case, however, his natural sense of family responsibility meant disobedience to God.

One definition of rebellion is "reserving the right to make the final decision." The firstborn, because of his self-reliance and natural leadership abilities, is an expert at this kind of rebellion. ("I know you told me to be home by eleven, *but* . . . "; "I know what God said, *but*. . . . ") In many cases, as in Abram's, the reasons on the "but" side look so good that it is hard to recognize the disobedience as rebellion. And often, the firstborn's rebellion is concealed even from himself.

As the biblical account clearly shows, Abram's inward rebellion led to headaches and heartaches for him, and to tragedy for Lot. Only after Abram amd his nephew had separated did God show Abram the land He had promised him.

Abram's relationship to Lot illustrates another characteristic of the firstborn: loyalty. Like most admirable qualities, this is a virtue that can be carried to a fault. In Abram's case, it impaired his relationship with God and even with Lot, to whom he demonstrated exaggerated loyalty. It is also interesting that God made His covenant with Abram after the death of Terah. Because of his unbalanced loyalty to family, it was necessary for God to separate him from his father before he could follow God's plan for his life.

Just as it took Abraham a long time to fulfill the role to which God had called him—that of the father of a great nation—so it may take the Christian firstborn a long time to overcome his conformity to the expectations of those to whom he is loyal, and to become the person God has called him to be. The firstborn's loyalty to his family can lead to bondage; his loyalty to friends can blind him to their faults and thus impair his ability to help them.

Both these problems came into sharp focus when two firstborns in our fellowship were engaged to each other. Patrice found it hard to "leave father and mother"—especially her mother, who has been the dominant influence in her life—in order to "cleave" to her husband-to-be. Brian was so loyal to his friends—especially to some of the younger men whom he had nurtured in the faith—that he sometimes forgot his first loyalty to his intended wife. Many similar cases have shown that the strong ties firstborns have to people in their past will make it difficult for them to give the undivided loyalty that a marriage partner should have.

Another firstborn trait that made trouble for Abram was self-reliance. The habit of relying on one's own abilities and reason makes it difficult to walk by faith and depend solely on God. Being unsure of God's protection, Abram was afraid he would be killed by a ruler who desired his beautiful wife, Sarai. Not once but twice he told her to say she was his sister.

Sarai was Abram's half-sister, so this wasn't a complete lie; it just wasn't the whole truth.

As Abram neared the century mark and was still childless, he began to doubt God's promise to make his descendants as numerous as the dust of the earth (Genesis 13:16). He fell back into the pattern of taking matters into his own hands and, at Sarai's suggestion, slept with the handmaid, Hagar, who bore Ishmael, his first son.

Thirteen years later, God changed Abram's name to Abraham, and restated His promise to make him the father of many nations (Genesis 17:4). But Abraham believed his son Ishmael was the one through whom his descendants would come. He actually fell down laughing when God promised him a son through Sarah, who was then 90 years old. Neither he nor Sarah had grasped the fact that nothing is "too hard for the Lord" (Genesis 18:14).

The miracle of Isaac's conception and birth through Sarah must have taught Abraham, at last, that the only responsibility of a child of God is to "trust and obey," a lesson that comes hard to many firstborns. The Abraham who unhesitatingly obeyed God's command to offer up this miracle son as a burnt offering is a far cry from the old Abram who lied, manipulated and outguessed God. His before-vacillating faith had now grown to such proportions that he believed "that God was able to raise [Isaac] up, even from the dead" (Hebrews 11:19).

In the last chapter we discussed the "dethronement" of the first child, which usually leads to another characteristic reaction—jealousy toward the "dethroning" younger sibling. In the case of Cain, the firstborn of all firstborns and referred to in Genesis 4 as a "tiller of the ground," this jealousy was long-lasting and brought about the tragic murder of his younger brother, Abel. Dr. Karl König comments:

The curse pronounced upon Adam when he was driven out of Paradise resounds in [this phrase]: "Cursed is the ground for thy sake; in sorrow shalt thou eat of it all the days of thy life; thorns and thistles shall it bring forth to thee; and thou shalt eat the herb of the field." This stern condemnation that accompanied Adam's departure from the Garden of Eden is handed on to Cain. The latter inherits his father's guilt and has from then onwards to carry it himself. The first born son becomes the bearer of the curse laid upon his father. He has to work the ground and redeem it by the labour of his hands.[1]

Abel's world was totally different: he was a "keeper of sheep." These different occupations suggest the contrasting temperaments of the first- and second-born of all mankind. Abel was apparently more passive, inward, content to dwell and dream among the flocks. Cain, on the other hand, seems to have been aggressive and extroverted, subduing the earth by the "sweat of his face" (Genesis 3:19). Firstborn Christians, like Cain, often try to serve God by the sweat of their faces rather than the power of the Spirit.

The Bible relates that both brothers presented to the Lord an offering—Cain of the fruit of the ground, and Abel of the firstlings of his flock. But when God accepted Abel's offering and rejected his older brother's, Cain became very angry.

Genesis does not tell us why Abel's sacrifice was more acceptable, although the writer of Hebrews attributes it to Abel's faith (Hebrews 11:4). Scholars have also suggested that God had already given Adam and his sons instructions concerning the type of sacrifice that was acceptable to Him— namely, a blood sacrifice.

Whatever the case, Cain did not see the problem within

himself; he saw only Abel, that threatening "dethroner," as the cause of his being rejected by God. God tried to get Cain to face his sin and recognize his responsibility for it, asking, "Why are you angry? . . . If you do well, will you not be accepted?" (Genesis 4:6-7, RSV). In other words, "Cain, if you obey My commandments and come to Me in the right spirit, you too will be accepted. My rejection of your offering has nothing to do with your brother."

Sadly, Cain refused to heed God's warning against the "sin couching at the door" (verse 7), and made no effort to master his jealousy. In anger, he carried out the "death wish" that so many firstborns have toward the sibling who has dethroned them.

Even if jealousy does not lead to overt violence, it is a serious block to the Spirit-filled life. "For while there is jealousy and strife among you, are you not of the flesh, and behaving like ordinary men?" (I Corinthians 3:3, RSV). If not destroyed completely and replaced by love, jealousy will lead to strained relationships, striving, character assassination and slander—not the peace that God intends for both natural and spiritual brothers.

In most cases, the firstborn's jealousy toward his younger sibling(s) exists side-by-side with feelings of love, yielding confusion or ambivalence. As Edith Neisser says,

> The roots of the older child's jealousy go deep, but the roots of his affection are equally far reaching. Parents might as well be prepared for both the older one's affection and his anger. Both pride and resentment toward the baby and also toward his mother for bringing such complications into his life will undoubtedly appear. The opposing feelings which ex-

ist side by side in human beings affect every relationship.[2]

Only the Spirit of God can set a person free from the sin of
jealousy, and allow ambivalence to be replaced by true,
wholehearted love for brothers and sisters.

When I asked the firstborns in our fellowship to read the
parable of the Prodigal Son (Luke 15:11-32) and tell me how
they felt about the elder brother, most of them said they
identified with him and felt the father was unfair. After all, he
had been the obedient and responsible son.

The "it's-not-fair" attitude is typical of firstborns. Studies
have shown that they work harder at pleasing their parents
than the other children do, and they feel their efforts should
be rewarded. "Elder brothers" in the family of God often
resent God's gracious, unmerited favor to some backsliding
brother or sister whose penitence seems to receive a greater
reward than their own good works. Reward for effort is the
world's philosophy—but it doesn't hold true in God's Kingdom, where salvation is "not of works, lest any man should
boast" (Ephesians 2:9, KJV).

After reading the parable, Maxine—the oldest of six children—related this unhappy scenario.

"While I was in high school, I got a part-time job to help take
some of the financial pressure off my parents. Underneath it, I
really wanted to win their approval. But it backfired, and
things only got worse between us. My mother seemed to
resent my helping out. Besides that, she and Dad centered
most of their attention on my younger [third-born] brother,
who was a problem child. It was almost as if he got approval
for his bad behavior," said Maxine, her voice straining, "while

I always stood in the background looking for a word of praise."

No wonder she identified with the elder brother! It is unfortunate that so many parents, like Maxine's, give the lion's share of attention to the rebel in the family, while ignoring their more conforming children. The resentment created in these obedient, responsible children may smolder for years before coming to the surface. In the case of the parable's elder brother, the resentment surfaced when he heard that his father was giving a feast for the penitent prodigal. The Amplified Bible's version of Luke 15:28 says that "he was angry—with *deep—seated wrath*" (italics added).

"Deep-seated wrath" in dutiful children could probably be avoided if parents were more observant of a child's good behavior and more liberal with their praise. Children, like adults, need to know they are appreciated.

In our meeting in the family room, Linda made a comment on the parable of the Prodigal Son that pinpointed a final major problem of the firstborn: *legalism.* The older brother had wanted to punish the younger brother for not obeying all the rules their father had set down. So he "punished" him by not running out to greet him.

"I remember 'punishing' my younger sister in various ways for not obeying," Linda said, "because I always obeyed my parents. Of course, inside I was rebelling against the rules. But if *I* had to abide by them, so did she!"

The legalistic attitude of most firstborns springs from two sources. One is the fact that their feelings of self-worth depend on their achievement, including the "achievement" of obedience. For the oldest child, achievement and acceptance go hand-in-hand. The typical firstborn, like the elder brother, looks to his actions rather than his heart attitude for proof of his sonship. As he said,

> "Lo, these many years *I have served you, and I never disobeyed your command;* yet you never gave me a kid, that I might make merry with my friends. But when this son of yours came, who has devoured your living with harlots, you killed for him the fatted calf!"
> (Luke 15:29-30, RSV; italics added)

For the responsible, achievement-oriented eldest child, accepting salvation by grace is often terrifically difficult. Many times he spends the rest of his life working hard to prove he was worthy to be saved.

Another source of the firstborn's legalism is his respect for authority. Adler offers an explanation for this attitude:

> Sometimes a child who has lost his power, the small kingdom he ruled, understands better than others the importance of power and authority. When he grows up, he likes to take part in the exercise of authority and *exaggerates the importance of rules and laws.* Everything should be done by rule, and no rule should ever be changed; power should always be preserved in the hands of those entitled to it.[3]
> (italics added)

Because of this dependence on rules and laws, it is easier for the firstborn to walk by the letter of the law than to walk by faith.

## The Blessing of the Firstborn

True, we found many problems faced by firstborns in our group, and in the accounts of Cain, Abram and the "elder brother." But the firstborn's unique position and characteristics also carry with them a great potential for blessing—both for himself and others. It was not mere whim that led God to select Abraham, a firstborn, to be the father of His chosen people. The very name *Abraham* makes us think of faithfulness and loyalty. To some degree, each firstborn brings faithfulness and loyalty into the family of God. The conservative, conforming nature of the oldest child contributes stability to his spiritual family and to his natural family.

Yielded to God, the jealousy of the firstborn can be turned to the sort of jealousy attributed to God Himself—deep care and affection for His children and a desire to see that they don't turn from their highest good to pursue less worthy goals. The firstborn may feel a similar sense of responsibility for his family, and he often becomes a very loyal and caring member of a church, assuming the role of parent figure in the family of God to whom others often turn as an understanding mother or father.

By the grace of God, the self-reliant, legalistic firstborn will finally be turned into a man or woman of faith. It should be encouraging to every firstborn to see what a prominent position is given Abraham in Hebrews 11, that great chapter on faith. God has forgotten all his weaknesses, and each step in Abraham's life is recorded as a step made "by faith."

So take heart! Those very weaknesses that are a problem in your Christian walk can become, by the power of the Holy Spirit, your greatest strength. Your name, like Abraham's, may one day be included in God's "Hall of Faith."

# Chapter 5

# The Second-Born

The weekend was perfect for a reunion among friends as we met at a sparkling blue lake in Michigan. Three of "us girls" were sitting on a pier, dangling our feet in the water and watching sailboats drift by. Quite naturally, the conversation came around to our children.

Celeste shook her head. "It's hard to believe that my two girls belong to the same family. The oldest is so disciplined and responsible, while her sister is so easygoing and irresponsible."

We chatted there in the sun for some time, with Celeste wondering how two sisters could be so opposite. Her descriptions echoed Charles McArthur's study of the first- and second-born children in two generations.[1] Recording the parents' descriptions of these children, he found that certain adjectives were used over and over in both generations.

First children were described consistently as *adult-oriented, conscientious, serious* and *studious,* which supports similar studies (as we have seen earlier). Second children were described most often as *not studious,* but were frequently said to be *cheerful, placid* and *easygoing.* How do we account for these reasonably consistent differences?

Part of the explanation, no doubt, lies in the attitudes of

their parents, both before and after the child's birth. We already looked at the high-key anticipation of most parents awaiting their first child. When the second baby is on the way, both mother and father are different people. Gone are the anxiety, fear and excitement they experienced before. Now initiated into parenthood, they are more relaxed and less eager for the arrival of child number two. It's not surprising, therefore, that this baby is usually more placid and less demanding than its older sibling—at least in the beginning.

According to Alfred Fischer, the problems of the second child usually begin between one and three years of age— about the time he becomes fully aware of the existence of a bigger, stronger rival vying for his parents' affection. Dr. Fischer carried out a study of two- and three-child families in which the two oldest children were of the same sex. He found that behavior problems and emotional disturbances were most prevalent among the second-borns, and that problems occurred most often when the second-born was of the same sex and close to the age of the first. Possibly the mother, fearing to neglect her firstborn, concentrates all the more attention and affection on him after the arrival of the second baby.

Dr. Fischer also found that when the second sibling is of the same sex as the first, the parents may feel disappointed, leading to an unconscious rejection of the second-born. The grandparents, too, may cherish the older sibling at the expense of the relatively uninteresting newcomer in his or her crucial early years.

The second child often receives far less than his share of the mother's time. These maternal manifestations of rejection, according to Dr. Fischer,

may be revealed in such commonplace phrases as

"The second is no bother at all," or "I'll certainly let this one cry more," or "I may have spoiled my first but I'm taking no chances of this with the second." . . . Aggravating the situation may be the perceptive older child, who, sensing his mother's preoccupation with him, communicates his importance and self-confidence to his younger brother, thereby intensifying the second's feeling of an inferior status.[2]

Small wonder that many second-borns have deep feelings of rejection!

Paradoxically, many mothers may later overprotect this second child, especially if he is also the youngest. In her study of 46 pairs of siblings who were the first- and second-born in their families, Joan Lasko found that the mother "did tend to baby, protect, and be solicitous of the second child to a greater extent than the first."[3]

Is it possible that eventual overprotection, which seems to be a manifestation of love, however misguided, could still lead to feelings of rejection in the child? My own experience gave me a clue.

My parents put tremendous pressure on my older brother to achieve and become a responsible adult. Perhaps because I was the first girl as well as the second child, they adopted a more permissive attitude toward me. I was not pushed to assume the responsibilities my brother was given, but was allowed to develop at my own pace.

The unfortunate result was that I evaded most responsibility as I was growing up, and became selfish and lazy. I was allowed to spend far too many hours reading and lounging around, growing up in a fantasy world in which Mother was always there to do what I neglected to do, or to cover for me when I needed an excuse. Although she was motivated by love, I subconsciously interpreted her lack of discipline as rejection.

*I don't have my brother's potential,* I thought. *That's why Mom and Dad don't push me. They don't love me as much as they do Tom, because I'm only a girl and they don't feel I can handle responsibility.*

The mother's tendency to baby her second child may begin in response to the firstborn's aggressiveness toward his younger sibling, or perhaps to compensate for her own earlier neglect of the undemanding second-born infant. Before long, a pattern has developed: push the first child toward achievement and responsibility, and protect the second child from the consequences of his irresponsible behavior.

One study of children's attitudes toward schoolwork, for example, showed that firstborns accept more responsibility for their own progress than do their younger siblings.[4] Children born later tend to blame others or circumstances for their failures. One of the most difficult things a second-born has to learn as a Christian is to accept responsibility for the consequences of his own actions—something he may never have had to do growing up.

As is the case with any birth order, the effects of being a second child depend in part on the size of the family and the sexes of the other children. Since I am not presenting an exhaustive study of all sibling combinations, I will simply mention the various possibilities. Readers interested in this subject may want to consult the references given in the bibliography.

## The Two-Child Family

Lucille Forer found two conditions emerging with fair consistency in the two-child family:

The younger is placed at a competitive disadvantage with the older, more powerful sibling. Or, the younger . . . becomes the parents' favorite, because he or she adopts different tactics from the more demanding older child. The second born quickly learns several adaptive techniques. One of these is to take advantage . . . of parental protection against aggression from an older brother or sister. Another is learning the art of compromise. Third is the development of more devious ways to satisfy needs. Whereas the older brother or sister may exert direct force to reach a competitive goal, the younger child learns to run plays around the end instead of bucking the line.[5]

According to Dr. Forer, the boy-boy family usually produces intense rivalry, and the *younger brother of a brother* is at a great disadvantage. All his life the younger boy lives with a rival who is older, taller and stronger, and one who usually excels in schoolwork. Many second-born sons, instead of attempting to compete with an older brother who is intellectually superior, develop into fine athletes. If the older brother excels in both these areas, however, the younger boy may withdraw from active competition, becoming unaggressive, quiet and easily discouraged.

This latter response is the one adopted by Tom, a second-born member of our fellowship. His older brother, Don, was an excellent scholar and a good athlete, too. From Tom's point of view, Don could do everything better than he could. As a result, Tom became quiet, introverted and easily discouraged. Although he is now a grown man with a family of his own, these traits are still evident in his personality.

The younger brother of a sister who is either motherly or domineering may not develop strongly masculine traits, and will probably remain relatively passive as an adult. However, says Dr. Forer,

> If the younger brother of a sister is permitted to be assertive, he will probably become self-reliant and nonconforming, and care little about what others think of him. He is likely to have high self-esteem, but may retain characteristics like tenderness and the ability to communicate, because he had two "mothers." He also may become domineering with women.[6]

Walter Toman describes the *younger sister of a sister* as more feminine than the firstborn girl, who may be too bossy. The younger sister, he says,

> is more likely than the older one to become the parents' darling, particularly her father's. The older sister is expected to obey the parents, to identify with them, to renounce her wishes in favor of the younger child.[7]

Most psychologists conclude that the *younger sister of a brother* occupies a very comfortable position in the family, and that this birth order has advantages for both children. The older brother's determination to maintain his status as number one will emphasize his masculinity, while the younger sister will usually capitalize on her femininity and grow up enjoying her role in life. She will probably also learn to look up to her brother, says Dr. Toman, accepting his protection, care and leadership, and adapting easily to making a home for her own family later on.

If the parents show too much partiality to their son, however, the younger sister may resent being stuck with all the household chores and may wish that she too had been a boy. In such cases, the desire to be more like her brother may lead to some rejection of her feminine role.

## The Three-Child Family

When my third child was born, the oldest was still two. For several months I had three babies in diapers. Because my second child, Shannon, was the quietest and least demanding of the three, she never received her share of attention in early life. I can easily understand, therefore, why the problems of the second child are likely to be aggravated by the arrival of the third. Having neither the privileges of the youngest nor the rights of the oldest, he feels "squeezed."

Many middle children resort to extreme behavior patterns in order to get the attention that has been denied them. Lucille Forer points out that in a survey of three-child families, children and their teachers both agreed that middle children appeared most prone to maladjustment, even though their parents did not favor one sibling over another.

Dr. Forer also found that this center birth position has a more adverse effect on girls than on boys:

> A middle boy among three boys usually is less anxious than either of his siblings, while the middle among three girls may be more serious, depressed, self-reproachful, and anxious than either of her sisters. . . .
>
> In adulthood, the middle of three girls is likely to reflect her lifelong attempt to gain attention and the dissatisfaction shown by her parents because she was not a boy. (The parents' favorite child is *least*

likely to be a daughter both preceded and followed
by a girl.)[8]

It may be of more than passing interest that, as Forer observes, both Joan Baez, the crusading folk-singer, and Kate
Millett, the angry philosopher of the women's liberation
movement, are the middle girls of three.

Fortunate is the middle child who is the only one of his or
her sex in the family. Research indicates that any child who
holds this position in the family possesses automatic distinc-
tion and usually grows up with high self-esteem.

According to Margaret Lantis, a social anthropologist
whose findings are cited by Charles McArthur, the common
denominator for *all* later-born children is "relative insen-
sitivity to adult scolding and relative isolation from adults."[9]
What distinguishes the second-born from later children is his
uniqueness in having only one child between him and the
parents. This one child ahead of him serves as what Alfred
Adler calls a "pacemaker," stimulating him to compete. While
the first child's eyes are on his parents, the second child's gaze
is riveted onto that older brother or sister.

From this imposing challenge, two remarkably different
patterns emerge among second-borns: placid and easygoing,
or hyperactive and pushy. The first type is seen more often in
the second of two children; the latter, in the middle child of
three. Both personality types emerge from the second-born's
perception of his "pacemaker" and the resulting competition.
If the first child is aggressive and demanding, the second
often "competes" by adopting a placid, easygoing manner. If,
however, he feels that his older sibling can be overtaken by
direct competition, he may become hyperactive and pushy in
his attempt to conquer.

As long as the second child feels that his method of competing, whether direct or indirect, is satisfactory, he will continue in this role. If the older sibling appears to be unbeatable, however, the apparently placid type of second-born may begin a retreat into neurosis, while the hyperactive, pushy type may become an outright rebel.

Because he sees himself as being in competition with the eldest child, the second-born tries to discover that child's weaknesses and to compete in those areas. For this reason, the second child usually appears to be the direct opposite of the first. The second-born boy who follows a serious, studious older brother may develop into an athlete or clown. The second-born girl whose older sister is "Mother's little helper" may seek to win her father's approval by becoming a tomboy.

Lucille Forer quoted a statement by Alfred Adler that was of particular interest to me:

> The worst position that the second child can be in, is to have an older sibling who is brilliant.[10]

My position exactly! My older brother not only has a brilliant mind, but is gifted musically and artistically. Since Tom was studious and artistic, I became a clown and a tomboy. Keeping house and having babies was another area in which Tom couldn't compete—so after my marriage I went overboard trying to prove myself in that department.

My refusal to engage in open competition had an interesting effect on my dream life: I dreamed continually of running—always running but never arriving. Whereas oldest children often dream of falling, second children, according to Adler,

> often picture themselves in races. They run after trains and ride in bicycle races. Sometimes this

hurry in his dreams is sufficient by itself to allow us
to guess that the individual is a second child.[11]

And so it is that the second-born may be either dreaming or
pushing himself toward some high goal. True, there can be
real problems if one is pursuing the wrong ends. But as long
as our goals are God-centered, the outcome will be true fulfillment, as the lives of Bible's great second-borns demonstrate.

# Chapter 6

# The Dreamers and the Racers

As a second-born, I feel a strong empathy to the "dreamy," number two child described by Karl König who

> listens to the voice of his sentiments and feel-
> ings. . . . His interest does not lie with the earth and
> her needs and destiny. . . . He likes to live without
> making too much effort. Existence does not only mean
> sweat and labor; it is joy and bliss, experience and
> wonder.[1]

His words recall a scene that played itself over and over in my childhood home.

Mother would set a platter of steaming chicken in the center of the white tablecloth. The others, having set out the plates, cups and silverware, began unfolding their napkins, sniffing hungrily at the basket of warm dinner rolls.

"Dinner's ready, Barbara!" Mother called patiently, as she filled the serving bowls with savory vegetables. But my chair remained empty.

"Barbara!" Mother's voice was a little sharper. "Where is that child? Someone go and find her."

Meanwhile, I was charging across a hot, sandy beach, the wind singing past my ears, flecks of golden sunlight sparkling off the ocean waves and dazzling my eyes. Beneath me, champing and shaking his handsome jet mane, was the most wonderful black stallion. And this desert island was our kingdom.

"Hey!" My brother's face, thrust through the bedroom door, startled me. The lapping waves were gone, and the stallion's masterful stride. The book slid from my hands onto the bed like forgotten reins. "Everybody's waiting for you *again*. And Mom's not too happy."

I slipped into my seat at the table, aware of the reprimanding eyes. But how could I explain my flights of fancy that were so real they swallowed up hunger pangs and calling voices? It seemed useless, and I never tried.

As early as Genesis, we find descriptions of firstborn and second-born characteristics. We already looked at Cain and Abel, Jacob and Esau. As we saw, Cain's work as a "tiller of the ground" fit the aggressive, extroverted personality of a firstborn. Abel was a "keeper of the sheep" and dwelled alone with the flock—an occupation ideally suited to a dreamy, introverted second-born.

The descriptions of Esau and Jacob offer the same contrast. Esau, the firstborn, was a "skillful hunter, a man of the field"; he was the rough, outdoors, he-man type—hairy, coarse of speech and given to sensual appetites (which proved to be his downfall). Jacob, on the other hand, "was a quiet man, dwelling in tents"; he was more thoughtful and knew what his brother's birthright really meant—and how to get it for himself.

Since the firstborn's pattern of behavior is usually outgoing and aggressive, the second child tends to "compete" for his place in the family constellation by becoming quiet and genial. Seeing his older brother or sister in verbal conflict with their parents, the second child may react against this behavior and try to win his parents' approval by adopting a "good child" image. James Bossard says that second children seek recognition, not by wresting control outright from their older siblings, but by making themselves agreeable or personally charming.[2]

Anyone who sets out to make himself agreeable necessarily represses many negative emotions. Thus, the repression of anger, hate, competitiveness and jealousy becomes a way of life for many second-borns.

Returning for a moment to my own experience, I saw my older brother erupt in frequent angry tirades, and thought how foolish he looked. I determined to keep my anger to myself instead of exposing my emotions in such childish outbursts. Negative emotions were "bad," so I began to deny that I even felt any anger, jealousy or bitterness. My self-control gave me a sense of superiority to my brother in at least one area.

As the years passed, repression became a way of life for me; it also became a cage. Inside was the real me, imprisoned in the false image I had created for myself. Every now and then, when the mounting pressure of repressed emotions became too great, I would explode in a wild, tempestuous fit of anger. Then, shocked and guilt-ridden after such an outburst, I would draw the remains of my agreeable image around me like a tattered quilt and retreat into its security.

Psychologists and psychiatrists have long suspected that continued repression leads to physical illness. I saw how dramatically repression can effect an individual's health in the case of Jean, a friend and neighbor of mine long before we became Christians in the same fellowship.

Jean was the second of four children. Her older sister had a violent temper, often causing arguments and shouting

matches. Jean, following the typical second-born pattern, became the agreeable and obedient child. As an adult, she was
known in our neighborhood as a quiet, "good" wife and
mother. So we were all surprised when her salesman husband—an aggressive, talkative man—walked out on her and
their three girls. Jean's emotional control as she went about
the job of raising her daughters without a father was incredi-
ble, and I greatly admired her strength.

Several years ago, in the midst of a stressful situation, Jean
began to have menstrual irregularities. A short time later, at
age 45, she suffered a heart attack. During her convalescence
she became, in the words of her children, "a different person—demanding, strong-willed and angry." After her recovery, however, she returned to her quiet, introverted de-
meanor.

Shortly thereafter, Jean joined our fellowship. She was a
passive member, sitting quietly through church and Bible
study. Then, suddenly, when she was again faced with a
stressful situation, her menstrual problems recurred. Medical
tests indicated the presence of malignant cells. Again, Jean
seemed to be the picture of self-control, though we all saw the
twinge of fear in her eyes.

And then one day she surprised us, her Christian brothers
and sisters, with a desperate cry for help. We all sat close to
her, listening, as she poured out a flood of anger, resentment
and feelings of rebellion—emotions that had been bottled up
for years. Gently, we encouraged her to face these emotions
for the first time, and to let the Holy Spirit cleanse her. At
length, she was again composed.

"You know," she said after a brief pause, "it's frightening for
me to face all those feelings—the hurt and anger that just came
pouring out of me right in front of all of you. But James 5 says
we must confess our sins if we want to be healed—and I do!

You can't imagine what a sense of lightness and relief I feel, now that I don't have to pretend anymore. Now I can face whatever comes."

Only two weeks later, new medical tests revealed absolutely no trace of abnormality! Her menstrual problems had stopped, too. The specialist was dumbfounded and had no explanation. But Jean did. She had faced her long-buried sin and confessed it to God. Now her emotions—and her body—were free from its deadly effects.

## A Meeting of the Masks

Our meetings with second-borns were vastly different from the time spent with firstborns, who were each so eager to have their say that we could scarcely tear away the microphone. The obvious thread that bound together the second-borns—myself included—was that we repressed our emotions. The first meeting, in fact, found us staring at each other with expressionless eyes, each repressing what we felt and thought! Once the ice was broken, we had to admit that repression was a major problem for each of us.

As the group members opened up to each other, Dave told how repressing his emotions had led him into the sin of hypocrisy. His older brother had become quite a rebel, and would use foul language in his arguments with their parents that shocked Dave. In the typical pendulum-swing of the second child, Dave's way of winning his parents' approval and offsetting his brother's actions was by becoming "religious." To keep his outward mask intact, he never showed such temper as his brother did, nor did he ever use foul language during his adolescence.

But years of repression caught up with him recently, when he and his brother fell into a heated argument.

"I was so shocked by what came out of my mouth," Dave admitted, shaking his head. "Later, I even denied to myself that I'd said those words."

He had almost gotten himself to truly believe he was innocent, until his brother reminded him of the quarrel and repeated Dave's words in front of their father. Now there was no hiding the anger and sin he had tried for years to conceal; it was out in the open. He had to confess that he was guilty of the same sin for which he had been condemning his brother. Even more than that, he had to face the reality that his pious pose was a facade, and that it was just as unacceptable to God as his brother's rebellion and vile language. At last he was able to enter a deeper, truer faith.

Dave's story actually posed a touchy question: what does a Christian do about negative emotions? Do we accept the advice of many modern psychiatrists who say, "Let it all hang out—give full expression to those emotions aroused by the unkindness and thoughtlessness of others?" How *do* we handle negative emotions, if not by repressing them?

As our group discussion progressed, another word began to surface: *transparency,* the exact opposite of repression. Transparency means that we give up our "agreeable" mask and risk letting others know our true thoughts and feelings. This can be a true healing process in the Christian community, if we take the time with each other to deal positively with destructive emotions like anger, resentment and rebellion.

From a loving but objective perspective, our Christian brothers and sisters can help us to recognize those personality traits in our lives that need to be corrected, and can give us scriptural insights that will enable us to deal with negative emotions. We can also communicate to each other God's forgiveness, and pray for strength in weak areas.

The highest incidence of delinquency, according to an article in the February 11, 1979, *Family Weekly*, is among second children in three- and four-child families. The eldest child often goes through a rebellious period and is more likely to engage in verbal conflict with his parents. Yet he has the greatest respect for power and authority, and often exaggerates the importance of rules. When his rebellious period is over, he will in most cases become a staunch defender of the status quo. Thus, since the second child tends to be the opposite of the first, it is not surprising that second-borns often have little respect for authority.

Adler held that the second child

is usually a rebel; authority is unlikely to have any charms for him, and he is more likely to egg on his younger brothers and sisters against the eldest and the parents, than to do much conventional governing on his own.[3]

We tend to view rebellion in terms of conduct—and in many cases it does boil out in angry or defiant action. Rebellion is essentially an attitude of the heart, however, a disdain both of rules and of those in authority. Even when unexpressed in words or actions, it is still a sin (see Matthew 5-7).

All of the second-borns in our group, even the quietest, admitted that they deeply resent direct orders given by someone in authority; they want to be asked politely to do something. None of them had ever recognized this resentment as a manifestation of an inner attitude of rebellion. Unless God intervenes, the second-born may go all through life being agreeable and never seeing the sin in his heart.

We still haven't explained why so many second-borns become outright rebels. Perhaps, in many cases, these children follow superior siblings. According to Adler,

> a "model" eldest may set so high and severe a pace by his dazzling qualities plus his privilege as a first born, that his second out of sheer despair at coping with such superiority may become either an extremely naughty and difficult child or even run off the rails altogether.[3]

The Prodigal Son is a good example of a juvenile delinquent—a second child who, as Adler put it, ran off the rails. It must have been difficult to follow an older brother who *never* disobeyed his father's commands (see Luke 15:29) and who, as they both knew, would come into the majority of their father's wealth. Perhaps this knowledge was partly responsible for the younger brother's desire to get his share while his father was still alive.

The impatience of the Prodigal Son is a common attitude of the second child, though it too may be repressed. It may stem from a feeling of having been cheated in life by coming in second—being an "almost-made-it." In the second children studied by Adler, he found an attitude akin to the envy of poor people, containing overtones of feeling slighted. Perhaps from a fear of being further slighted, the second-born wants what is due him *now.*

This feeling of having been cheated in life helps to explain the high incidence of delinquency among second-borns. People who feel they have been cheated are more likely than others to "cheat" in return—to resort to illegal means, sometimes even violence, in order to obtain what they think society owes them.

In the last chapter I mentioned two types of second-borns:

placid and easygoing, or hyperactive and pushy. These two types both stem from the same root cause: the second child's perception of his "pacemaker," the firstborn. If he views his older sibling as unbeatable, he will become discouraged, give up the competition and become, to all appearances, placid and easygoing. Or it may lead to rebellion and delinquency. On the other hand, the second child who feels that he may be able to overtake the first will often become extremely competitive.

In some cases, the second-born will stay more or less immobilized by discouragement all through his life. In any group situation he will find a "pacemaker," and then compare himself with that individual—in most cases, unfavorably. Such comparisons are made even within the Christian family.

Laura is a quiet, retiring brunette who has never had much to say in the meetings of our fellowship. She explained the reason for her timid nature to the rest of us second-borns. Accustomed to a superior firstborn sister as a pacemaker, she picked a "superior" member of the fellowship as her pacemaker and ended up as she always had—discouraged.

While Laura made this confession to our group, I looked around at the 21 second-borns and realized that, except for three or four, they were all relatively inactive members of the Body. Each one had a great deal to offer; but most of them, feeling unable to compete with the pacemakers they had chosen, retreated into quiet and inactivity.

A second-born who is struggling with this kind of inferiority syndrome needs to realize that the Body of Christ suffers when any person in it is noncontributing, since God has a particular function for every member.

*Rivalry* between members of the Body can be equally damaging. The second-born who is extremely competitive and pushy will choose a pacemaker and then seek to surpass that person by fair means or foul. The fruit of such competitiveness is one church member criticizing another, or even making slanderous insinuations about Christian brothers or sisters. Certainly every Christian—whether or not he is a second-born—must guard against and ask God to redirect that competitive spirit.

Many second-borns do not recognize their competitiveness, since they compete only in those areas where they are assured of winning. Second-borns are experts in spotting weaknesses in their pacemakers and using those weaknesses to their own advantage. Unlike the firstborn, whose loyal spirit (as shown in Chapter 4) may blind him to weaknesses in others, the second-born may use the weaknesses he discerns to justify *dis*loyalty.

In the preceding chapter, we saw that one of the adaptive techniques of the second child is the use of more devious ways to satisfy needs. Jacob, the younger twin of Esau, was a master in this.

The struggle between these brothers apparently began in the womb, and we know that from his birth, Jacob was pressing on the heels of his twin, trying to overtake him. Hence, the name Jacob, which means "he supplants" or "he takes by the heel."

Jacob had the second-born's characteristic ability to spot weaknesses in his older sibling. By capitalizing on Esau's sensual appetites, Jacob manipulated his brother into exchanging his birthright for some hot soup. His mother, Rebekah, knew that God's plan was for the elder brother to serve the younger (see Genesis 25:23), but she wasn't willing to leave it to God to carry out His plan in His own time and His own way. She schemed with Jacob to defraud Esau of his firstborn's blessing from their father. The result was bitter enmity between the two brothers.

While trying to escape Esau's vengeance, Jacob had his first encounter with God in the wilderness. Appearing to him in a dream, God promised to make Jacob's descendants into a great nation and to give him the land on which he was lying. But even after this startling dream, Jacob made a vow in which he tried to manipulate God:

> If God will be with me, and will keep me in this way that I go, and will give me bread to eat and clothing to wear, so that I come again to my father's house in peace, then the Lord shall be my God, and this stone, which I have set up for a pillar, shall be God's house; and of all that thou givest me I will give the tenth to thee. (Genesis 28:20-22, RSV)

*If* God fulfills the conditions laid down by Jacob, *then* he will worship Him as God and will give Him a generous ten percent commission on all blessings. What a pathetic attempt to twist God's arm!

At Haran, God used Laban to discipline Jacob and give him a dose of his own devious medicine. After working seven years to win Rachel as his wife, Jacob was tricked into marrying her older sister, Leah. In order to obtain Laban's permission for his marriage to Rachel, he had to promise his father-in-law another seven years of labor. Yet even twenty years of God's discipline under Laban did not cure Jacob of his devious ways. By outscheming his uncle and father-in-law, he managed to acquire great wealth before taking French leave.

Jacob finally met God face-to-face at Peniel. They wrestled

there until daybreak and, amazingly, God "did not prevail against Jacob" until He touched the place of his natural strength—his thigh. Then Jacob, the supplanter, became Israel, the one who had "striven with God and with men, and . . . prevailed" (Genesis 32:28, RSV).

Jacob's severest disciplines still lay in the future: the death of his beloved Rachel and the loss of his favorite son, Joseph (who had, unknown to him, been sold into slavery). Toward the end of his life, we find some evidence that God's pruning and discipline had finally begun to produce "the peaceful fruit of righteousness" (Hebrews 12:11) in this devious, wrestling man.

When Jacob, now an old man, decided to go down to Egypt to see his beloved Joseph, he first offered sacrifices to God and received His promise to be with him on the trip (Genesis 46:1-4). The old Jacob would have made his plans and departed; the new Jacob sought God's will in all things.

The story of Jacob should encourage every second-born Christian. If God could transform Jacob the schemer into Israel the patriarch, He surely can help us to fulfill the function he has for us in His family.

The redeeming characteristic of the second-born is his ability to repent and change direction, as illustrated in the story of Jacob; and, more dramatically, in the New Testament story of the Prodigal Son. When the full impact of his deplorable condition hit this profligate rebel, he could say,

> I will arise and go to my father, and I will say to him, "Father, I have sinned against heaven and before you; I am no longer worthy to be called your son; treat me as one of your hired servants."
>
> (Luke 15:18–19)

For the achievement-oriented firstborn, it is difficult to accept the grace of God as a gift. Not so with second-borns; for us the gospel of grace is tailor-made. We have been engaged all our lives in an uneven competition, and it's a great relief to learn that God's acceptance is based on what He has done for us, not on what we can do for Him. In God's Kingdom, there are no "second-bests," no "almost-made-its."

I theorize, based on my own experience, that a second-born will always need a pacemaker to call forth his best effort. The Christian second-born would do well to choose as his pacemaker some godly person whom he admires, whether contemporary or ancient. If his response to this pacemaker is a desire to imitate rather than compete, such a person can set a needed pace for the second-born and encourage him to persevere until he has "finished the race" (II Timothy 4:7). Paul encouraged his converts to use *him* as a pacemaker: "Brethren, join in imitating me, and mark those who so live as you have an example in us" (Philippians 3:17, RSV).

I have dared to choose the Lord Jesus Christ as my Pacemaker, since the Bible tells me that I am being conformed to His image (Romans 8:29). Like Paul, I recognize how far I am from attaining His perfection; but "I press on toward the goal for the prize of the upward call of God in Christ Jesus" (Philippians 3:14, RSV).

I am still competitive, and perhaps will always need a pacemaker to spur me on; but God has turned this weakness into strength. That competitiveness keeps me running with perseverance the race that is set before me (Hebrews 12:1), and my Pacemaker in this race is also my Coach, my Friend and my Lord, Jesus Christ.

# Chapter 7

# The Third-Born

Two parents and two children provide an enormous number of variables, each exerting a kind of gravitational pull in the family constellation. Consider the possibilities of age variance, temperaments and male-female mixtures. And when a third child is added to this group, all of whom have their fixed orbits already, the variables affecting him or her become exponential. As a result, little research has been done on this birth position, and little has been written about it. From a statistical standpoint, the third child is perhaps the stranger, the mystery child, the outsider.

Personally, I have had ample opportunity to conduct my own research in this area: I have been married to a third-born for twenty years, and I am the mother of a third-born son. Still, the scarcity of written source material almost forced me to skip over to a chapter on youngest children. But with John's encouragement, I added to my "sample of one" fourteen other third-borns, hoping to unlock the secrets of this "mystery child."

Karl König says,

> From his start in life onwards, the third child is a stranger. There is first of all the rather far away sphere of the parents. Then follows the other layer

occupied by the first two siblings, and at last there is the third, the lonely child.[1] (italics added)

To clarify König's position, let's consider the emotional climate in a given family at the time a third baby arrives. Mom and Dad were excited and anxious over the birth of their first child, who soon became their pride and joy. They were less tense in preparation for child number two, although the mother might have been concerned about her ability to care for more than one baby. Then she learned that she could look after a younger child without destroying the ego of the first. Somehow, everything worked out; it was silly to worry.

When the third baby is born, there is nothing to get excited about. His arrival in the family hardly creates a stir. The parents most likely feel that he will find his niche without too much effort on their part.

And by this time, the first two children have established a relationship with each other. The birth of the third child may be a fascinating distraction for them at first, but they are likely to lapse back into familiar routines fairly quickly. Little wonder that the third child can grow up feeling like a stranger, an outsider in a home that seems to function as easily with or without him.

Such was the situation in my own family. My two oldest children, John and Shannon, had established a good working relationship before Tom, my third-born, was old enough to participate in their activities. John was always the leader: he decided what to play, where to play it, and whom to play it with. Shannon was the perfect follower. She never argued, but reinforced John's leadership by agreeing with all his plans.

When Tom was old enough to enter this arrangement, complications set in. Unlike his older sister, Tom was a fighter. He expected his plans to get equal time, and felt the rub when they didn't. Shannon became a "buffer" at times, trying to keep an uneasy peace between her warring brothers. Like a typical middle child, she became adept at this. As with other trios of children, mine often regrouped, John allying with Tom against Shannon.

Even in a situation like this, however, the first is merely *using* the third to help defend his position against child number two. The third is merely a handy ally for the oldest, not his intimate companion.

How does this feeling of not belonging affect the third-born? When I asked the group in our family room this question, Scott spoke up immediately. "I always *enjoyed* being alone, even as a kid," he said.

It was surprising to hear this likable young man assert that he "really didn't need to be with people."

Scott wasn't alone. One after another, the third-borns told how they had learned to amuse themselves as children, without needing the companionship of a playmate or parent. To some degree, at least, third-borns seem to be more self-sufficient than their two older siblings—at least within the context of the family. They may become less dependent on their parents or siblings for approval.

They do, however, seek approval elsewhere. Consequently, according to Dr. Bossard, third-born children have a tendency to turn from the family to the community, becoming socially oriented and socially ambitious.

These characteristics—self-sufficiency and community orientation—did not seem to me to fit together at first. I had only to look in my own family, however, to see that they did work together with fine symmetry.

Tom has always struggled to find his footing with John and Shannon. He was forced, in a natural way, to become self-sufficient. And yet that struggle has equipped him with a compassion that may one day thrust him out into the community to serve others.

## Loneliness

The need to "belong" in the larger community, if not at home, may grow from a deep-rooted sense of inferiority. According to Karl König,

> The loneliness of the third child . . . bears the sting of inferiority. The child longs to take its place among other people, yet lives under the firm impression that the others are not concerned with its existence and do not care to make its acquaintance. . . . [They may] withdraw into their own being and build a fence or even a wall against the hostile world, or they gather their strength together and after having done so, break out and try to conquer by force that which otherwise would not yield to them.[2]

I have observed, especially in our sample group, that it is not always an either-or situation; third-borns may use withdrawal or force alternately, depending on the circumstances.

The majority of the third-borns in our group said that they withdraw when they feel rejected. Unlike the second-born, who withdraws because he can't conquer, the third-born withdraws because he has always felt like an outsider, and it is natural for him to be alone. Even in the middle of a crowd, the third-born has a sense of not belonging. "It's strange," said one woman. "I remember feeling lonely growing up, even though I had a large family and a lot of friends."

The "force" that third-borns employ is more likely to be

mental than physical. They usually learn to control temper by the time they are mature, and compete with their wits instead of their fists. Our group of third-borns was the most boisterous group we had met with so far, and also the funniest. We soon realized that humor was a device to cover up their feelings of inferiority.

I recalled comments that various teachers had made in the past about our son Tom. "He's so *funny*," one had told me, "and when I try to discipline him, he just makes me laugh." Tom was on his way to becoming the class clown when his dad and I realized a potentially serious problem was developing. Tom was so busy conquering through his wit that he was neglecting his schoolwork. Today, though Tom still has a keen sense of humor, he has learned to discipline himself in school.

We have seen that the first child has his roots in the past, and, as a result, tends to be conservative and traditional. The second child lives in the present and has a tendency to do what "feels good" now. The third child senses that his destiny lies beyond the family, and therefore becomes forward-looking.

All of our third-borns recognized themselves as future-oriented, often envisioning their success in some future setting. The majority said they almost never dream at night. Evidently their daytime fancies fulfill their desires in such a way that they are not aware of working out problems in their sleep.

The tendency to daydream often gets the third child into trouble with teachers and parents. One of the women at our meeting said that a teacher had told her mother that her attention span was about three minutes. She confessed to us that she was always imagining what she would do after school that day—even if it was still early morning.

This future orientation can give third-borns an optimistic

outlook and even a humorous approach to the present. Many in the group admitted that they react with humor even to crisis situations. Some felt that the humor springs not from a lack of concern but from their optimistic attitude that "everything will be all right." Typically, their response was, "It will soon pass."

The discussion about future orientation also shed light on another facet of the typical third-born's personality. I have always envied my husband's ability to accept God's forgiveness for sin as soon as he has confessed it. Every Christian, of course, is entitled to claim this instant and complete forgiveness, but many are unable to do so without a struggle.

The fortunate third-born lives in the future and has a conveniently short memory. Usually he can receive God's forgiveness for past and present sins and then forget he ever committed them.

This lack of concern about the past and the present can lead to problems, however. The third-born may have a very lenient conscience. Many in our group admitted it had been easy for them to lie to their parents. One man said he could tell a lie and, five minutes later, not even remember what he had lied about. Martha said she rarely felt guilty about the wrong things she did. "I was a good liar, too, and wasn't really bothered if I broke the rules."

Because he is not saddled with an overactive conscience, the reborn third-born is able to enjoy his freedom in Christ. If all Christians were third-borns, it's possible that Paul would never have had to warn the Galatians not to nullify God's grace by falling back into bondage to the law. A lenient conscience can be an impediment to acquiring the discipline needed for a life of holiness. But the third-born whose life is controlled by the Holy Spirit will not be tempted to use his freedom for license.

His sense of being forgiven can draw him closer to God with a thankful heart—a far cry from "good works" or "cheap grace."

So the third-born may have a true advantage. He may be closer than the rest of us to discovering that meekness of heart Jesus talked about in the Sermon on the Mount. He knows his past failures, but is not bound by them. And he may realize that apart from a close union with God the Father he will not reach any of his longed-for future goals. And it is only through a meek subjection to God and His power that any of us will "inherit the earth."

This, I soon discovered, is proven again and again by some of the Bible's most outstanding third-borns.

# Chapter 8

# The Power of Meekness

Before any of us can come into a true, close relationship with God, we must undergo a deep, deep change in the heart—a turning from our ways to His ways. For many third-borns, it is often hard to see the need for this kind of change. After all, if your life isn't "too" bad, why change it? This is the first, biggest hurdle that keeps many people from knowing God.

When my husband made his first commitment to Christ, I remember his saying, "I like my life the way it is. I don't want to change." Although he prayed the sinner's prayer and confessed Jesus as his Savior, there was no true repentance, and things stayed much the same.

John feels that his real rebirth took place about a year later, after much exposure to the Word of God. Gradually he realized that no one, regardless of his "goodness," is acceptable to God on his own merits. This brought a true conversion of the heart, and since that time John's life has changed radically.

Like John, many people are happy with their lives and have no burning desire to change. But being satisfied with yourself is only self-righteousness, nothing more. When you open yourself to God's Holy Spirit, He will make changes, conforming you to the image of Jesus Christ. That *does* make a difference! And I have found that nothing instills this desire to change like seeing God's Spirit at work in the life of another person.

Mary, a third-born in our fellowship, described her experience this way: "I asked Christ to take over my life—at least, I said the words. I didn't really think I needed to change. After all, I was a pretty good person. But seeing the change in my husband's life, and in the lives of other Christians, made a big difference. It gave me the desire to know Christ as they seemed to, at a deeper transforming level." At that point, Mary realized that "good enough" was *not* enough.

Since the third-born is one of the more practical persons in the family constellation, they are more likely to be convinced by actions than words. There is a lesson here for all of us, especially for spouses of unbelievers. To the third-born, seeing is believing. He wants to see the reality of a changed life. The best way to win him to Christ, therefore, is to let your character and actions speak louder than mere words.

Once a conversion of the heart happens, the power of God can begin to work in extraordinary ways. As a practical-minded person, the third-born may turn his attention outward, making himself a willing vessel for God to use in bringing change to tough and serious problems in the real world.

## A Reluctant Leader

Such was the case with Moses, one of the greatest third-borns in all of Scripture. We are told that Aaron was three years older than Moses (Exodus 7:7), and that Miriam must have been at least five or six years older, since she was responsible to watch over Moses when their mother hid the infant in a basket at the edge of the River Nile (Exodus 2:4). Many people are not aware that his early formative years were spent with his brother and sister in his own home (Exodus 2:9), even though he was later raised as Pharoah's grandson.

Moses was 80 when God called him to lead His people out of Egypt. But in spite of his chronological maturity, Moses was reluctant to accept this responsibility:

> "Who am I that I should go to Pharaoh, and bring the sons of Israel out of Egypt?"
> (Exodus 3:11, RSV)

> "But behold, they will not believe me or listen to my voice . . . "
> (Exodus 4:1)

> "Oh, my Lord, I am not eloquent, either heretofore or since thou hast spoken to thy servant; but I am slow of speech and of tongue." (Exodus 4:10)

> "Oh, my Lord, send, I pray, some other person."
> (Exodus 4:13)

As might be expected, leadership comes more naturally to the firstborn than to the third-born, since the latter is seldom the leader in his childhood home. Abraham and Moses exemplify this difference between first- and third-borns. When God called firstborn Abram to leave his country in order to become the founder of a great nation he didn't argue; "Abram went" (Genesis 12:4). First children expect to be leaders and to do great things; but it is not so with the third child.

Moses' difficulty in assuming leadership began in his own household with his wife and children, when he apparently failed to follow the Abrahamic covenant and circumcise his son (Exodus 4:24-26). God made it clear that Moses could not be His deliverer until the covenant condition was fulfilled; and

Zipporah, Moses' wife, had to perform the circumcision, much against her will.

Reluctance to exercise authority as head of the family is a common failing of third-born husbands. In the pre-Christian era of our marriage, John, just to keep peace in the family, often let my arguments and complaints persuade him to go against his better judgment. In many household matters, especially where the children were concerned, I was definitely the authority. Like most third-borns, John withdrew from the field of battle when he saw conflict coming; he preferred peace at almost any price. For this reason I saw him as weak, especially when I compared him with my strong-willed first-born father.

Only God could have straightened out the relationship between my husband and me, and I thank Him that He has brought His order into our family. Now that John has taken his place as the head of our home and I have accepted his authority, the children are much more willing to accept my authority.

The third-born Christian needs to ask God to enable him or her to face conflicts and work them out under the guidance and in the power of the Holy Spirit.

That Moses possessed his share of stubbornness is shown by his persistence in arguing with God about his call to leadership. Even after a face-to-face encounter with God—who answered each objection Moses could raise and even equipped him with miracle-working power—Moses stubbornly refused to accept God's assignment. His stubbornness finally aroused the Lord's anger, at which point He agreed to let Aaron, the "eloquent" second-born, serve as Moses' spokesman (Exodus 4:14). By his refusal to trust God with the control of his mouth, Moses lost a great blessing.

Yet God's power is made perfect even in our weakness (II

Corinthians 12:9). Having no faith in his own leadership ability, Moses had to develop tremendous faith in God. When the
people of Israel were trapped between the murderous Egyp-
tians and the waves of the Red Sea, Moses commanded them
to stand firm and "see the salvation of the Lord, which he will
work for you today" (Exodus 14:13, RSV). At the point of
desperation, Moses was forced to trust God completely.
    God's response was intriguing:

> Why do you cry to me? Tell the people of Israel to
> go forward. Lift up *your* rod, and stretch out *your*
> hand over the sea and divide it, that the people of
> Israel may go on dry ground through the sea.
> (Exodus 14:15-16, italics added)

In effect, God was reminding Moses that the power to
provide a means of escape had been placed in *his* hands.

The hot temper displayed by Moses in his earlier life is
another third-born characteristic. In anger, he had even killed
a man (Exodus 2:11-12). We see it in Levi, the third son of Jacob
who, along with his brother Simeon, killed all the males in
Shechem to avenge their sister Dinah (Genesis 34:25; 49:5-7).
David's third child, Absalom, killed his eldest brother, Amnon, to avenge his sister, Tamar (see II Samuel 13:1-29). It is
interesting that all three of these third-borns killed to avenge a
hurt done to someone else. Perhaps they saw themselves as
God's personal avenger. Of these, however, only Moses allowed God to turn the weakness of anger into the strength of
meekness.
    Anger and meekness are exact opposites, the one excluding
the other. William Barclay says that the Greek word translated
*meek* "describes the man, who in loving and obedient humility

accepts the guidance of God and the providence of God, and who never grows resentful and bitter about anything which life may bring to him, in the certainty that God's way is always best, and that God is always working all things together for good. [He is not the one] who is *self-controlled* . . . but the man who is *God-controlled*."[1]

When Moses finally learned to trust God with the control of his life, he became the meekest man "on the face of the earth" (Numbers 12:3, RSV).

Nearly a decade ago, *The Journal of Psychology* published the findings of a group at Rhode Island College investigating the birth order of Carmelite nuns. Not surprisingly, they found that a disproportionate numer of third-borns became nuns. The meekness of the third-born girl, coupled with her tendency to withdraw, seems to predispose her to this kind of vocation.

Meekness is a beautiful quality that seems to be demonstrated best by third-borns. Whereas first- and second-borns are prone to grasp for control or power over people, third-borns are reluctant to accept such power, even when God gives it to them. Moses' meekness was never more evident than when his leadership was threatened, first by Miriam and Aaron, then by Korah and his followers.

It's not hard to understand why firstborn sister Miriam, who had cared for Moses as a baby, felt that she should have an equal voice in leadership. Aaron, that agreeable second-born, went along with her, just as he did with the people when they begged him to make them gods to lead them (Exodus 32:1). Second-borns don't like to swim against the tide. The fact that only Miriam was punished for this insubordination shows us whom God held responsible. Instead of being resentful of Miriam's jealousy, however, Moses pleaded with the Lord to heal her (Numbers 12:13).

When Korah and 250 leaders of the congregation challenged Moses' leadership, the latter did not attempt to defend his position. Instead, he let God decide the outcome of this power struggle. Time after time, Moses interceded to save the rebellious nation of Israel from God's avenging anger (Exodus 32:30; 33:12-16; Numbers 16:41-50).

I have emphasized the meekness of the third-born for a specific reason. Because of the characteristics associated with their birth order, many third-borns are ideally suited for leadership roles; yet their meekness can keep them from becoming leaders. As their brothers and sisters in the Christian family, we can encourage them in their God-given abilities and talents.

## Unfulfilled Promise

Without God's direction and control, the third-born can never realize his potential for leadership and may never achieve his goals in life. Karl König says,

> The third child is a person who has the greatest difficulties in achieving his aim. He flowers quickly but also withers away rather rapidly. A third child is often full of a promise that is hardly ever fulfilled. He is a child who reaches out too high and has too short a time to attain his goal. [2]

Although Moses neither flowered quickly nor withered away rapidly (we read in Deuteronomy 34:7 that at age 120, his "eye was not dim, nor his natural force abated"), even he failed to obtain his goal. How heartbreaking it must have been for him to stand on Mount Nebo and gaze into Canaan, the Promised Land, knowing that he would not be allowed to lead his people across the Jordan. Because of disobedience to God's orders, the Lord had told him that he would die on that mountain, at the very entrance to the land that had been his goal throughout forty years of nomadic existence.

What was the sin that led God to punish Moses so severely? At Kadesh, God had commanded him to speak to the rock and order it to produce water. In his *anger,* Moses spoke to the people rather than the rock. With his rod he hit the rock twice, saying, "Hear now, you rebels; shall we bring forth water for you out of this rock?" (Numbers 20:10, RSV). By striking out— with his rod and with angry words—he let out an inner anger that was festering.

I can't help believing that this fatal slip, when Moses' meekness forsook him, originated in his stubborn refusal to let God take control of his mouth forty years earlier (Exodus 4:10-13). What a lesson for each one of us! Whatever we do not yield to God may someday prove to be our undoing, standing between us and the fulfillment of God's plan for our lives.

Still, Moses' meekness is displayed again in his acceptance of God's punishment. Only once did he ask the Lord to allow him to go into the Promised Land (Deuteronomy 3:23-26). When God refused, Moses accepted even this great disappointment with no trace of bitterness. After his death on Mount Nebo, the Lord honored him by giving him a private burial in a place which is not known to this day (Deuteronomy 34:6).

Jesus' own words point to the tremendous reward for meekness: "Blessed are the meek, for they shall inherit the earth" (Matthew 5:5, RSV). William Barclay explains how this Beatitude is fulfilled: "To have the discipline of meekness is to have the power which makes life great, for only when a man has mastered himself is he able to rule others."[3]

Empowered and controlled by the Holy Spirit, the third-born can learn to overcome his weaknesses—such as anger and stubbornness—and assume his inheritance as a leader of God's people.

# Chapter 9

# The Last-Born

Just like the third-borns, our sample group of youngest children were divided into two distinct personality types. The majority were talkative, bubbly and enthusiastic; but a few were withdrawn and shy.

That youngest children do fall into these two distinct categories has been reported in the literature on birth order. Researchers have found a correlation between these personality types and the predominance of either second-born or "only child" characteristics. A statistical study reported in 1970[1] showed that last-borns who have a sibling close to them in age are more like second-borns, aggressive and striving. Where there is a large age gap between the two youngest children, the last-born is apt to be more like an only child— shy, quiet and somewhat withdrawn.

According to Rudolf Dreikurs,

> The youngest child resembles an only child in many respects; but in others his position corresponds to that of the second born, and accordingly he develops a considerable urge to put himself forward. His efforts to outdo all the other children may be remarkably successful. Since he has to use a whole bagful of tricks to mask his situation as the

smallest of the family, he often becomes quite inventive and adroit.[2]

A major factor in deciding the personality type of the last-born child, predictably, is the attitude of other family members toward the "baby." If they suppress him, as Lucille Forer points out, he may develop a low self-esteem; whereas, affirmed, he will develop a healthy one.

Unlike his brothers and sisters, the youngest child has no successors, only "pacemakers." For many years—in some cases, all his life—he is the smallest and weakest member of the family. As Alfred Adler says, "No child likes to be the smallest, the one whom one does not trust, the one in whom one has no confidence. . . . " Hence, says Adler, the youngest child often sets out "to prove that he can do everything. His striving for power becomes markedly accentuated and we find the youngest very usually a man who has developed a desire to overcome all others, satisfied only with the very best."[3]

Such a child is like the second-born in his desire to overtake his pacemaker—or, in most cases, pacemakers. Last-borns of this type *earn* their title of "King Baby" or "Baby Boss."

On the other hand, a youngest child who is dominated and teased excessively by the older siblings may decide it is hopeless to try to overtake his pacemakers. Withdrawing from the power struggle, he becomes shy and lacking in self-confidence. Such a last-born may remain, in the words of Alfred Adler,

> cowardly, a chronic plaintiff forever seeking an excuse to evade his duties . . . a veritable "alibi artist" who attempts nothing useful, but spends his whole energy wasting time. In any actual conflict he always fails. Usually he is to be found carefully seeking a

field of activity in which every chance of competition has been excluded.[4]

## Coddled, Protected—and Insecure

Our visitor had just arrived, and I slipped a mothering arm around the shoulders of our youngest daughter, Kelly. To my own chagrin, I heard myself introduce her: "And this is my baby."

Kelly, who is eleven years old, winced. I didn't even have to look to see the unhappy grimace on her face. Only days before, she had asked me pointedly *not* to refer to her as "my baby" any longer.

Why is it that mothers, myself included, don't want to stop babying their youngest children? More serious is the question, What effect does this babying have on the child?

The last baby, whether third- or twelfth-born, has parents who are a good deal more experienced (therefore more assured and relaxed) than they were when their first child was born. One would expect that this child would be the most secure member of the family. Unfortunately, he is often the *least* secure. The reasons for this are many: overprotection and a lack of discipline on the part of the parents, combined with teasing, exclusion or protectiveness on the part of the older siblings.

In some cases the last child is unplanned, even unwanted; and may be regarded by the whole family as a burden. This attitude is most prevalent when the other children are much older, and especially when the last child is a "change-of-life" baby. It sometimes happens, usually in large families, that an older sibling is given the principal responsibility for the care of this youngest child. While such an unwanted baby can become the darling of the family, the influence of prenatal and early postnatal rejection hardly increases the child's sense of security.

Almost any combination of the factors discussed above may be responsible for the fact that the youngest child is usually the one who receives the least amount of discipline, especially from the male parent. Partly, perhaps, because of her husband's relative lack of interest in the "baby," there can be a special closeness between this child and the mother. In many cases, the mother strongly suspects that she will have no more children. It is hard to gauge the psychological impact of this knowledge. In addition, some mothers try to atone for all the sins committed with their older children.

Another important factor is that the "baby" is usually spared the demand for achievement put on the older children, particularly the firstborn. Because there are so many older and more powerful people in his world, the last-born child may not have to assume much responsibility. This, along with the lack of discipline, can account for the fact reported by Lucille Forer that youngest children are often more spontaneous, original and creative.[5] They may also be allowed to remain immature, which will later cause their insecurity and sense of inferiority to mushroom.

Problems with verbal communication: A youngest child often retains a subconscious desire to remain dependent. This desire may reveal itself in the retention of immature speech patterns, or "baby talk." Other speech problems, such as stuttering, may develop because the youngest child is trying so hard to get in his "two-cents' worth" when his older brothers and sisters are talking.

Another verbal hangover from babyhood is the habit of screaming for parental assistance. Only recently did I realize how often Kelly still manipulates me by screaming. In the past, I have responded immediately to her cry for help (after all, she is the "baby") and disciplined whatever sibling was responsible for upsetting her. Now that I recognize her screaming as a manipulative technique, I try to stop and assess the situation before handing out punishment. In most cases I find that Kelly is responsible for getting herself into hot water.

Yet the youngest child does need parental assistance in obtaining justice at the hands of older siblings. When she was about six, Kelly began to show signs of real hostility and inferiority feelings. The other children were then ten, eleven and twelve. Soon I became aware of what they were doing to her. Dinnertime at our house is a time for sharing the events of the day. But whenever Kelly told about something she had experienced, her story was greeted with expressions such as, "Oh, that didn't really happen," or "Big deal!", or, "You're just exaggerating again." Everything she tried to say was made to seem unimportant—or, worse, untruthful.

The youngest child tends to exaggerate in order to stress the importance of what he has to say. This tendency is a sign of insecurity, and to accuse him of lying aggravates the problem by increasing his insecurity. When I explained to my older children that their "put-downs" were actually causing Kelly to exaggerate, they began to give her equal time and greater respect.

The need to be taken seriously may be the basis for compulsive talking, and this need is especially great in youngest children. In its November 7, 1977, issue, *Newsweek* carried an article entitled "A Lastborn Speaks Out—At Last," in which the author expressed the need in this way: "If Firstborn's lifelong concern is power, *our* collective issue is the question of validation, the problem of being taken seriously."

A study of students at California State University[6] showed that first- and last-borns were the most talkative groups;

"only" and middle children were found to be relatively quiet. My youngest is rarely quiet. When her mouth stops moving, I usually put a thermometer in it to see if she is sick!

Parents must give equal listening time to all their children. Likewise, we should teach them that communication requires them to listen as well as to talk. Otherwise, there is a real danger that the "baby" will never feel he is part of the family, but will always remain an observer looking in. This feeling of not belonging, expressed many times by women who come to me for counseling, springs from insecurity and feelings of inferiority. Until these are healed, no individual can experience true, vital fellowship with Christian brothers and sisters.

Within the heart of every youngest child, believes Lucille Forer, there are two opposing needs—to retain the love of his family, and to develop a recognized strength and ability. In an effort to retain his parents' love, and to gain power over his older siblings, the "baby" resorts to tattling on his brothers and sisters, or spilling their secrets to his parents.

Kelly has done this so often that she is usually excluded when the other children are "talking secrets." Then she tattles on them for excluding her!

This habit of tattling can even carry over into adulthood. When a friend complained to me that one of her co-workers was always "running to the boss" with information about other members of the office staff, I asked if this woman happened to be the youngest in her family.

"Why, yes," replied my friend. "I happen to know that she is. But how did you know?"

In keeping with this tendency to tattle is Lucille Forer's finding "that laterborns are more likely to write family histories and autobiographies, thus perhaps divulging secrets and information their elders would like to keep hidden."[7]

Almost half-a-century ago, it was found that youngest chil-

dren scored lowest in a test designed to measure self-sufficiency.[8] In many ways, parents fail to encourage achievement
in their youngest children. Whereas parental pressure to
achieve falls heaviest on the firstborn, it becomes somewhat
lighter for each succeeding child. Further, the degree of interest shown by parents in their children's accomplishments
tends to decrease from the oldest to the youngest.

(Exceptions to these generalizations, as we noted in Chapter 3, are often found in relatively large families. Especially in
lower-class families, as Dr. Forer observes, the youngest child
may be the only one to have an opportunity for higher educa-
tion, and the parents are likely to stress the need for achievement in this child.)

We parents commit a sin against our last-born children
when we fail to encourage or discipline them, when we expect
too little of them, or when we allow the rest of the family to
serve them. This kind of upbringing is poor preparation for
life in a world which is unkind and intolerant.

Al is a young man in our group of last-borns, the youngest
of three boys. His new job as salesman requires self-motiva-
tion—a terrific responsibility. But he is having a difficult time
keeping regular hours. Since he doesn't have to punch a
timeclock or report to work at a certain hour, Al finds it easy to
sleep a little later or stay at home and watch TV instead of
going out calling on prospective clients. For the first time, he
must battle to do for himself what others have always done for
him.

Several married women in our fellowship are youngest
children. In the context of our group discussions, they admitted it was difficult for them to run their households efficiently.
When a youngest girl marries a firstborn, this inefficiency can
be a real point of conflict. The disciplined and responsible
oldest child has a hard time accepting irresponsibility in anyone, especially his wife.

The firstborn child, as a rule, is the one who has the greatest need for approval by his parents. The last-born seems to have a special need for love and esteem from his whole family. While this might seem to produce a child who is consummately agreeable, this is not so.

While the greatest proportion of problem children, according to Alfred Adler, is found among firstborns, the next-greatest proportion is found among the youngest. "The reason for this," conjectured Adler, "generally lies in the way in which all the family spoils them. A spoiled child can never be independent. He loses courage to succeed by his own effort."[9]

The youngest, whether boy or girl, is the one most likely to be tied to the mother's apron strings, whether he wants to be or not. From the Christian perspective, I see these "apron strings" as a spiritual umbilical cord that needs to be cut before the adult child can come into the fullness of his life in Christ. This is especially true in a marriage. Until both partners break that cord, it is impossible for the couple to experience the oneness that God intends.

Some time ago I sensed that my sister, Jeannie, the third and youngest in our family, needed to be released from a type of bondage to our mother. At that time she felt no such need, but promised she would be open for God to show her if such a problem existed.

Several months later Jeannie awoke one morning in a state of deep depression, for which she could not account. She began weeping, unable to stop. After her baffled husband left for work, Jeannie stood at the sink washing the breakfast dishes, her tears falling into the dishwater. The only "upheaval" in her life was this: Mother had left the state that very morning for a vacation in Florida.

Jeannie, a nurse, instantly recognized that she was suffering from a classic case of "separation anxiety," such as young children experience when they are separated from their mothers. And then she recalled our conversation of some months before. Silently she prayed, releasing Mother to the Lord and asking God to break the spiritual bondage between them. As mysteriously as it had come, her depression lifted.

Faith, an attractive, softspoken member of our group of last-borns, related another incident of parent-child bondage.

Vic, her husband, was a man much like her father, and for sixteen years their marriage was a parent-child relationship. When she needed spending money, for example, she would rely on her "little-girl" technique: "I'd act very shy and coy, the way I did when I asked my father for money. Then in my sweetest 'baby' voice, twisting my hands, I'd say, 'Vic, honey, could I have a few dollars?' Vic would respond by asking me sternly, 'For what?' Then I would have to account for the money, just as I did with my father when I was a child."

After Vic and Faith became Christians, he grew as the leader of a Christian community. But their relationship remained the same. It wasn't until they learned the scriptural meaning of oneness between husband and wife that they saw the need for a change in their marriage. It was a great relief to Faith when she discovered that God could change her dependence into strength. Asking Him to help her become a "grown-up woman," she renounced the childish tactics (coyness, pouting and temper tantrums) that she used to get her own way. At last she overcame her need for dependency and began to become the woman God had designed her to be. Faith and her husband now have a joint ministry to couples with problems similar to their own.

Bob, a Ph.D. and another member of our "last-born" group, is the fourth child of five. Yet he has the characteristics of a youngest child, since eight years elapsed before his younger sister was born. Bob married Susan, a girl with strong first-born traits, who is three years older than he.

In this marriage, Susan was the parent and Bob the child. Both continued their childhood patterns—Bob pouting when he didn't get his way and Susan being the mother who punished or rewarded according to her "child's" behavior. When they became aware of the God-ordained roles for husband and wife, they decided to let the Holy Spirit transform their relationship.

"It hasn't been easy," Susan admits, "but it's worth all the struggle and pain. I now have the husband I always wanted—a man who accepts the authority and responsibility God has given him as head of our home."

Not all youngest children, even those among the group who are basically shy and withdrawn, remain passive and dependent. The youngest of six, Peggy, told the group that she was largely responsible for five unsuccessful marriages. When I asked her what caused the breakup with each husband, she replied, "I was spoiled as a child. And I wanted to show my husband that I didn't need him or anyone else. Everything had to be my way—and when it wasn't, I left."

Two years ago Peggy had a dramatic encounter with Christ, reminiscent of the meeting between Jesus and the woman at the well. God has broken through her facade of independence, and she no longer has to hide her need for love.

Whenever you encounter a last-born, whether child or adult, who is swaggering around and looking as if he has the world by the tail, try to realize that beneath that brash exterior may beat a heart filled with fear and insecurity.

Alfred Adler says the spoiling of the "baby" can produce such feelings:

> All pampered children suffer from fear: it is by means of their fears that they can attract attention and they build up this emotion into their style of life.

They make use of it to secure their goal of regaining connection with the mother.[10]

More detrimental than spoiling, perhaps, is the overprotectiveness of most mothers toward their "baby." This overprotection, discussed earlier in this chapter, tells the child, "You are not capable." Mothers who were the youngest in their childhood families need to be especially on guard against their tendency to give their own children "smother love."

The youngest in a family tends to be the most volatile emotionally. Tears are never very far from the "baby's" eyes. Perhaps the teasing received by last-borns when they are growing up is partly responsible for the fact that they are also subject to outbursts of anger. Our youngest is highly sensitive to teasing, and I have observed this same attitude in many adult "babies."

Also, Forer's description of the youngest child as "charming, a good companion, playful and lighthearted"[11] seems to be borne out by a study made at the University of Southern California on the relationship between birth order and popularity among peers. Last-born children were found to be the most popular, firstborn the least popular, and middles somewhere in between.[12]

The firstborn's desire to dominate and "boss" makes him a leader but not a play partner. Middle children have learned to relate, more or less successfully, to both older and younger siblings. But youngest children, according to the California study, must develop their interpersonal skills—negotiation, accommodation, tolerance, and a capacity to accept less favorable outcomes—in order to learn to relate successfully.

As a rule, youngest children are delightful companions, if

one can overlook their irresponsibility and occasional outbursts of anger or longer spells of pouting. Every one of Kelly's
teachers since her kindergarten days has written a comment
similar to the one that appeared on her report card this year:
"Kelly is a joy to have in class."

# Chapter 10

# The Last Who Will Be First

The last-born child is blessed in his birth position, perhaps above all others. As Jesus Himself said, "Some are last who will be first" (Luke 13:30, RSV), and I believe this includes the youngest child who feels he is the least among his brothers and sisters. To me, the lives of Gideon, Joseph and David suggest that God can do exciting things through a youngest child whose way is committed fully to Him.

## From Coward to Hero

We first meet Gideon, the last-born son of Joash, in the sixth chapter of Judges as he is furtively threshing out wheat near his father's winepress. At that time Israel was at the mercy of the Midianites, a fierce tribe of nomadic people who for seven years had preyed ruthlessly upon them. Gideon was actually hiding in fear when the angel of the Lord found him. How ironic that the angel addressed him in verse 12 as a "mighty man of valor"! God, who has said that His "strength is made perfect in weakness" (II Corinthians 12:9, KJV), obviously saw the potential for great courage in this fearful man.

Still stunned, no doubt, by the angel's greeting, Gideon was told to "go in this might of yours and deliver Israel from the hand of Midian" (v. 14). Gideon must have wondered, *What might?* Like Moses, he began offering excuses: not only was his clan the weakest in Manasseh (one of the least-respected tribes of Israel), but he, Gideon, was the least in his family.

Unlike Moses, however, Gideon was willing to obey God, if only He would give him a sign. Perhaps in deference to Gideon's timidity, God gave him not one sign but four (Judges 6:17-21, 36-40; 7:9-14).

Gideon's impulsive generosity is characteristic of the youngest. He prepared a meal for his divine guest, offering him food that would have kept himself and his family from starvation for many days. After accepting and consuming Gideon's sacrifice, the angel disappeared, and Gideon found himself speaking directly with God.

That same night God gave further instructions to Gideon—instructions that are significant for all last-borns. He was to tear down his father's altar to Baal and cut down the idol totem pole planted beside it in honor of the goddess Asherah. In the last chapter we talked about the youngest child's strong dependence on his family for love and support, sometimes to his own detriment. In Gideon's case, God was rooting out dependencies and breaking wrong ties. Gideon was so afraid of the reactions from his family and the other men in the clan that he waited until nightfall and carried out God's command under cover of darkness. But the important thing is, he did obey God. By this act Gideon transferred his dependence from his family to God.

Breaking bondage to the family is a vital step in the life of any youngest child. Many last-borns are unable to make that break with their "family idol" so that they can place their total dependence on God. As long as they are more concerned with the good pleasure of their family, they will be unable to pursue God's plan for their lives.

But the last-born who is able to transfer his dependence from his family to God can accomplish great things in the Lord's power. That kind of dependence becomes his greatest strength. Timid Gideon was able to learn in one night the lesson it took Abraham, a self-sufficient firstborn, a lifetime to learn: total dependence upon God.

Once Gideon had learned this lesson, God was able to use him to win one of the most extraordinary victories in all of military history. At His command, Gideon released more than two-thirds of the soldiers from his volunteer army of 32,000. Then, still following the Lord's orders, he sent home another 9,700 men, leaving him with an army of just 300 to face the Midianite horde. God wanted Israel to know that they had been delivered by *His* hand and not their own might.

After requesting and receiving one more sign that the Lord was with him (7:9-15), Gideon was ready for battle. No arm-chair general, he instructed his men to "look at me, and do likewise" (7:17). This is also common of the youngest child—leading his subordinates by becoming their companion and friend, as well as their example.

Likewise, other interpersonal skills that the youngest child develops in his family relationships make him a diplomat *par excellence*. Gideon's confrontation with the proud men from the tribe of Ephraim called for all the diplomatic skill he possessed. Angry that Gideon had not included them in his army, they "upbraided him violently" (8:1). In a masterpiece of diplomacy, Gideon convinced these arrogant men that their "mop-up" operation was more important than his successful surprise attack. Apparently his personal charm and skill at negotiation defused a dangerous situation and placated his potential enemies.

The grateful Israelites wanted to make Gideon their king, but Gideon had no desire to rule. "I will not rule over you, and my son will not rule over you," he told them. "The Lord will rule over you" (8:23). Had he been a firstborn or a competitive second child, Gideon would probably have jumped at this opportunity to retain his position of leadership. The youngest in a family rarely has the chance to develop the mindset of a leader, however, or the desire to achieve recognition. In spite of the miraculous way God had used Gideon, he still had the deep-seated insecurity common to many youngest children.

Gideon did find some security in the gold that came to him from the spoils of war. Yet the youngest child is not usually materialistic in the strict sense, since he generally values people above things. Nevertheless, a basic insecurity can give him an almost desperate desire for the security represented by wealth.

When I shared this bit of information with our group of youngest children, it generated quite a bit of discussion. Most admitted that a savings account was so important to them that they were reluctant to spend money even for necessary items.

Doug, for example, confessed his tendency to "lean on money rather than the Lord. I guess that's one reason I lost my last job. God wanted me to depend on Him, not on money, for my security."

From the gold he had acquired, Gideon fashioned an ephod—a garment that became an object of worship for the Israelites. Gideon, who had once destroyed his father's idols, now established one of his own. Although this youngest child was able to depend on God in a remarkable way, he lacked the discipline necessary to continue as God's instrument. He had his moment of glory, and God allowed him to end his life in a tranquil and uneventful manner.

## From Last to First

Joseph is at the same time a youngest, only and oldest child. Although he had ten older brothers and one older sister, he was the first child born to Rachel, his father's favorite wife. Joseph's younger brother, Benjamin, was born only after Joseph had grown up as Jacob's youngest and Rachel's first and only child.

Joseph was the kind of last-born who has a deep desire to surpass all his siblings and gain power over them. This desire surfaced in his dreams, which he took pleasure in relating to his brothers.

> "Hear this dream which I have dreamed: behold, we were binding sheaves in the field, and lo, my sheaf arose and stood upright; and behold, your sheaves gathered round it, and bowed down to my sheaf." His brothers said to him, "Are you indeed to reign over us? Or are you indeed to have dominion over us?" So they hated him yet more for his dreams and for his words.
>
> (Genesis 37:6-8, RSV)

Joseph even dared to dream that his mother and father would bow down before him!

Although Jacob rebuked Joseph for his attitude of superiority, he was probably the one responsible for it. The Scripture records:

> Now Israel [Jacob] loved Joseph more than any other of his children, because he was the son of his old age. . . . But when his brothers saw that their father loved him more than all his brothers, they hated him, and could not speak peaceably to him.
>
> (Genesis 37:3-4, RSV)

As is often the case, Jacob's favoritism proved to be no favor to his son. Besides contributing to Joseph's feeling of superiority, it engendered jealousy and bitterness in the other children. Parents today still make the mistake of showing favoritism to one child—in most cases, the "baby." Almost inevitably the favored child is the one who suffers most in consequence of his parents' misguided love.

In cases where the older siblings also dote on the "baby," that child is likely to grow up with the erroneous expectation of being favored by everyone throughout life. Joseph's brothers, however, did not dote on him—and small wonder. Besides boasting about his dreams of superiority, he used the typical last-born tactic of trying to ingratiate himself with his father by tattling on his brothers (37:2). This added fuel to the flame of his siblings' jealousy. Eventually their hatred of this self-righteous younger brother became so great that they determined to get rid of him. When the opportunity came, they broke their father's heart by selling Joseph into slavery and then telling Jacob he had been torn to pieces by wild animals.

Parenthetically, it is interesting that Reuben, the firstborn, was the only one of Joseph's brothers who attempted to save him. As the firstborn, the one who should naturally inherit the birthright, Reuben was the one who had the most to lose from Jacob's favoritism toward Joseph. But the firstborn's protective and responsible nature won out over his jealousy. Reuben's greatest concern was to save his father the heartbreak of losing his favorite son.

The last-born child who is *not* the victim of favoritism has an unequaled opportunity to learn how to be a servant of God. It is a scriptural principle that we must humble ourselves before God can exalt us (Philippians 2:5-9; I Peter 5:6). The youngest child who accepts his inferior position in the family has a headstart toward acquiring the humility that will enable him to "count others better than" himself (Philippians 2:3).

Unfortunately for Joseph, his father did not give him the opportunity to accept his inferior position in the family; and only after God let him spend thirteen years in either servitude or prison did he learn humility. In Egypt Joseph became the slave of Potiphar, an officer of Pharaoh. Because the Lord was with Joseph, his master took an immediate liking to him and put him in charge of his entire household. Joseph must have been thinking, *I'm somebody's favorite again.*

Unfortunately, he was too much a favorite with Potiphar's wife, who attempted to seduce him. When Joseph tore himself from her clutches, she took revenge by having him thrown into prison. But the Lord was still with Joseph and "gave him favor in the sight of the keeper of the prison" (Genesis 39:21, RSV).

Nevertheless, Joseph spent more than two years there. Only when God knew that Joseph had mastered his thirteen-year lesson in humility and trust did He secure his release from prison and make him ruler over all Egypt, second only to Pharaoh.

Joseph's total trust in God is shown by the statements he made to his brothers when they were reunited: "So it was not you who sent me here, but God" (Genesis 45:8); and, "As for you, you meant evil against me; but God meant it for good" (Genesis 50:20).

The man who depends upon himself thinks that it lies within *his* power to control the circumstances of his life. The man who depends on God knows that nothing can happen to him unless God allows it, and that "in everything God works for good with those who love him, who are called according to his purpose" (Romans 8:28). Joseph had become a truly humble man—and for this reason God could exalt him.

## The Man After God's Own Heart

God sent Samuel to Jesse's house to anoint one of his eight sons as the next king of Israel. But the prophet had no idea that God had chosen David, the youngest, for this honor. Not until David's seven brothers had all passed before Samuel and been rejected by the Lord did Samuel even inquire about an eighth son—who, he was told, was out tending the sheep. What a beautiful example of God's delight in using the weak, the low and powerless (I Corinthians 1:27-28), and raising them to positions of leadership!

One of Dr. Toman's findings about the youngest brother of brothers is that he

> can be daring, bold, and fresh. He likes to challenge opponents who are stronger than he is. He tends to wager higher bets than others. If need be, he will even risk his life.[1]

Who proves this statement better than David? As a mere stripling, he dared to challenge Goliath, the boastful, murderous Philistine giant. No man had dared to challenge this terrifying foe!

When David came to visit his brothers, bringing provisions from his father, he arrived just in time to hear Goliath roar out his daily challenge to the host of Israel. David's immediate and brash question was, "Who is this uncircumcised Philistine, that he should defy the armies of the living God?" (I Samuel 17:26). Eliab, his oldest brother, responded with typical older-sibling contempt for David's bravado.

Someone paid attention to David's words, however—King Saul, who summoned the young boy to his aid. With the characteristic persuasiveness of the last-born, David convinced Saul that he was the man for the job.

Though David was brash, he was no braggart. He knew the Source of his power, and gave credit where credit was due: "The Lord who delivered me from the paw of the lion and from the paw of the bear . . . " (I Samuel 17:37).

David's refusal to wear Saul's armor further indicated his dependence on God. David would never have lied about his relationship to his wife, as Abraham did; he did not stoop to the cunning and trickery of Jacob; he did not even need the miracle-producing rod of Moses. David had God, and God was enough!

David's reply to Goliath's contemptuous challenge reminds us of Joseph's attitude toward his older brothers. David's confidence was not in himself, however, for he declared: "This day the *Lord* will deliver you into my hand . . . that all the earth may know that there is a God in Israel and . . . that the *Lord* saves not with sword and spear . . . " (I Samuel 17:46-47; italics added).

In his total dependence on the Lord, David is more like Gideon. But David was no impulsive one-shot hero destined to fade into oblivion. By accepting his inferior position in the family, David had learned two vitally important lessons during his adolescence: first, to be faithful and responsible in the little things of life; and second, to transfer his dependence from family and friends to God.

Given the lowly assignment of tending his father's sheep, David was no hireling running away when danger threatened. Out in the lonely stretches of grazing land, separated from any family and older brothers who might have done his chores and fought his battles, David had learned that he and God were a majority. The result was that he became "a man after [God's] own heart" (I Samuel 13:14).

Another characteristic of the youngest brother of brothers, according to Walter Toman, is that he tends to lean on other people, particularly men. Youngest children seem to have more need for friends than any of their older siblings. Partly because of this need and partly because of their skill in interpersonal relationships, they usually attract friends easily. In many cases, the unfortunate result is that they become more dependent on friends than on God.

There is yet another pitfall associated with the last-born's deep need for friendship. Sometimes his love for a friend may surpass his love for his spouse. In David's case, he seems to have valued Jonathan's friendship more than either of his marital relationships at that time. In his lament for Jonathan he wrote, "Your love to me was wonderful, passing the love of women" (II Samuel 1:26). Could it be that David's attraction to Bathsheba was due in part to the void left in his life by the death of his friend?

David, like Joseph, was thirty when he came into power. In the years that David was a king without a throne, God had matured him and taught him many things. He had learned to depend on God, not only for protection against his enemies but for the supply of his everyday needs. Twice God tested David by giving him an opportunity to kill Saul and seize the kingship (I Samuel 24:6 and 26:9). But David steadfastly refused to "put forth his hand against the Lord's anointed," even though he had already been anointed as Saul's successor. Knowing that God was in charge of his life, David could wait until God saw fit to give him the throne.

In his treatment of Saul, David serves as a living example of Toman's description of the youngest child:

> He tends to be kindhearted and soft. Even in the guise of an aggressor or a cynic, he shies away from the final consequences of aggression or sarcasm. He can forgive and forget.[2]

After Saul's death, David continued to demonstrate his forgiving and kindhearted nature by showing great compassion to Saul's descendants (II Samuel 9:1).

One incident for which David is remembered is his enthusiastic dancing before the Lord while he was clothed in little more than a loincloth (II Samuel 6:14, 20). In this impulsive action, David demonstrated the emotional freedom characteristic of youngest children. Can you imagine Abraham, Jacob or Moses dancing with such abandon, oblivious to the stares of the servant maids?

The last-born's emotional impulsiveness in this instance was God-directed; but when David later glimpsed the beautiful Bathsheba bathing on her roof, his impulsiveness led him into a series of sins which brought the curse of God on his family. God told David through the prophet Nathan, "Now therefore the sword shall never depart from your house, because you have despised me, and have taken the wife of Uriah the Hittite to be your wife" (II Samuel 12:10).

The circumstances that led David into the sins of adultery and murder should serve as a warning to every youngest child. An impulsive, pleasure-loving nature can trip up the last-born. Without discipline, a life full of promise and creativity may never achieve its full potential. This danger is much greater for the youngest than for any other member of the family constellation if they have been indulged as children.

What a price David paid for his impulsive act of adultery! The child of that union died, and Nathan's prophecy concerning the strife in David's house proved to be accurate. David's firstborn son, Amnon, raped his half-sister and was killed by his half-brother Absalom as punishment. Later, Absalom himself lost his life in an unsuccessful attempt to seize his father's throne.

In spite of his faults, however, David never wavered in his devotion or in his total dependence on God. When David fled for his life during Absalom's insurrection, the Levites brought the Ark of the Covenant out of Jerusalem. David made them return the Ark to the city, for he would not rely on anything but God to deliver him: "If I find favor in the eyes of the Lord, he will bring me back and let me see both it and his habitation; but if he says, 'I have no pleasure in you,' behold, here I am, let him do to me what seems good to him" (II Samuel 15:25-26).

David was guilty of murder and adultery, but his will was committed to walking in dependence on God. Knowing that he could not please God by his works of righteousness, he was able to repent and receive forgiveness through God's grace (Psalm 51). The youngest, like the third-born, knows what it means to walk in grace, free from the legalism that is such a hindrance to older brothers and sisters.

With this special childlike characteristic, the last-born has an advantage in his spiritual life. Jesus Himself said, "Unless you turn and become like children, you will never enter the kingdom of heaven" (Matthew 18:3). The trustful dependence so common to children can be a real asset to the last-born who, like David, directs that trust and dependency toward God.

The greatest danger to the youngest is that the undisciplined, impulsive nature of the child may persist into adulthood. If "all-work-and-no-play" is the problem of the oldest child, "all-play-and-no-work" may well be a pitfall for the youngest. Instead of encouraging this attitude in their last-born by pampering and favoring them, parents need to teach their youngest children discipline and help them to recognize that work is not a fate worse than death!

What a challenging opportunity the youngest child has to

become like David—a man or woman after God's own heart! Instead of hiding that dependent spirit under a guise of independence or mock courage, *face* it; learn to rely on God. Instead of resenting your inferior position in the family, accept it, knowing that the God who positioned you last desires to make you first.

# Chapter 11

# The Only Child

Along with the normal pressures and struggles of growing up, the only child is sometimes faced with a strange, silent kind of rejection from society-at-large. To this day, many old wives' tales and misconceptions about the only child persist.

And sometimes the rejection isn't so silent. Parents with only one child, for instance, are often urged by their families and friends to have another baby because "it isn't good for a child to grow up alone." Only children are also more likely to be treated badly by those who assume they must be spoiled brats just because they are only children. And if you treat someone badly long enough, you can be fairly certain they will begin to behave badly. Yet I've often heard adults excuse or explain a child's misbehavior by saying, with a knowing look, "He's an *only* child, so what do you expect?"

From my reading, I discovered how widespread this line of thinking is. One sampling of college students, according to an article in the May 1976 issue of *Psychology Today*, described only children as more unhealthy, self-centered, attention-seeking, dependent, temperamental, anxious, unhappy and unlikable than people with siblings. Alfred Adler, the pioneer in studies on birth order, even went so far as to say that such children "have difficulties with every independent activity and sooner or later they become useless for life."[1]

More recent studies reveal that there are definite advantages and strengths associated with this lonely position in the family constellation. Only children are not a group of weak neurotics. Like every other child in God's family, they possess a potentially valuable combination of strengths and weaknesses.

Because the conditions surrounding the birth of the only child are so similar to those associated with that of the oldest child—tense, anxious parents eagerly awaiting the arrival of their first baby—we would expect the personality of single children to be similar to that of firstborns. And to some degree it is. On the other hand, as Dr. Forer points out, it may also resemble that of youngest children, since the only child is the last as well as the first of his family. The only child, therefore, is an interesting and sometimes ambivalent blend of first- and last-born traits.

Parents of single children differ in several respects from the parents of most firstborns. For one thing, they tend to be older. Among the seven only children in our sample group, only Sandy was born to parents under 30, and she was the only one whose parents had *chosen* to have just one child. The other parents, for one reason or another, were unable to have more children. In many cases, the mother had difficulty in conceiving and carrying a child to term. Joan's parents had been married fifteen years before she was born. Gaye's mother was married after 30, and was 38 when her only child was born.

Studies have indicated that congenital defects are more common in only and youngest children than in first children followed by others.[2] Many parents, afraid of having a defective child, choose to have no more babies. Also, parents with a single child are often more anxious and overprotective than parents with two or more offspring. (One only child of our acquaintance says that, until he was 40, his mother was afraid he would die of a childhood disease.) The only child has no younger siblings to absorb some of his parents' anxiety and attention.

Adler, who may be responsible in part for the poor image of the only child held by psychologists, described the parents of such children as

> timid and pessimistic; they feel they will not be able to solve the economic problem of having more than one child. The whole atmosphere is full of anxiety and the child suffers badly.[3]

When I commented to our sample group that the physical health of an only child is a source of considerable anxiety for the parents, especially the mother, it drew an immediate response. Gaye's account, for example, was intriguing.

"When I was a small child, I remember picking up a cat and then rubbing my eyes. My mother yelled, 'You're allergic!' and immediately took me for allergy tests. Some time later I did develop an asthmatic type of condition."

When Gaye was about 16, her asthma became severe, often keeping her in bed for two weeks at a time. Because of her limitation, she was never able to participate in strenuous activities. About this time, Gaye became a Christian and joined our fellowship. I spent a good deal of time with her, as we tried to deal with her anger and rebellion toward her mother.

At the time, she was attending college, too, and in her gym class was required to run a mill—something she had never tried to do under the watchful eye of her mother. She wasn't at all sure she could make it, but she decided to try. "I still remember the feeling of elation when I crossed that finish line!" she told us, beaming.

Shortly after that, when Gaye was 21, her father developed a serious illness. As she prayed for him, she realized that she had no control over the outcome of his illness. And for the first time, she consciously admitted that she had tried to control her parents for years.

"I had always thought my mother controlled me," she explained. "And then the Lord showed me how much I manipulated both my parents. I would get what I wanted by going from one to the other until one of them gave in. I knew my mother was jealous of my close relationship with my father, and I used it to punish her for trying to dominate me."

With this realization, she released her father totally into the hands of the Lord. Shortly after that, his physical recovery began, and he and Gaye's mother came into a closer, healthier relationship than ever before.

Interestingly, Gaye's asthma attacks decreased, and today she is free from most allergic symptoms. She believes that several factors contributed to her healing: getting away from home, becoming a Christian, learning to accept and forgive her mother, and learning how to deal constructively with stress. The asthma, it seems, began as a response to her mother's suggestions, and then became a manipulative tool that helped Gaye get what she wanted, as well as protected her from stressful situations.

Bob—Gaye's senior by twenty years—responded immediately to her story: "I remember how, when I stubbed my toe or something, I would act as if I were in great pain just to get my parents' attention. I found I could almost control them by my physical complaints. Now, I realize, I overreact to small hurts in order to get attention from my wife." Very quickly, others confessed their use of physical pain to gain attention.

Gaye's story in particular illustrates the unnatural relationship that can develop between parents and an overprotected only child. In her case, she was trying to compete for her mother's place in the family. Likewise, a male child can develop a "mother complex," according to Adler, wanting to get his father out of the picture. Lucille Forer elaborates that the son and father may compete for Mother's attention, the mother and daughter for Dad's.

Some authorities believe that a satisfactory sexual relationship between the parents helps to prevent maternal overprotection. Where this relationship is poor, according to one study, the child must bear the brunt of the unfulfilled love life of the mother.[4]

In a family of three, relationships may be rather intense, and it is especially important that the parents have a good relationship with one another. Otherwise, according to Dr. Murray Kappelman, the family becomes a triangle,

> with both parents at the bottom and the only child at the peak. . . . The child . . . soon realizes the extent of his power. He will begin to manipulate his parents, putting them into direct competition for his favor and affection.[5]

For reasons that may or may not be related to this intense competition, only children have a greater propensity to homosexuality than children with siblings. Several studies have revealed that a preponderance of homosexuals come from either one- or two-child families. Male homosexuality, according to Dr. Bertram Forer,

> appears to have its roots in the relationship with the mother as the major model and source of gratifica-

tion as well as frustration. This may also apply to
lesbians. . . . The girl may receive the impression
that her mother would have preferred her to be a boy
or not to exist at all.[6]

These findings emphasize the importance of the Christian
family structure (see Ephesians 5:22-33) in the normal development of a child's sexuality as well as his character and
personality. Where the father is truly the head of the house
and the parents have a loving, balanced relationship with each
other, children have role models that help them to establish
stable marriages when they become adults.

Like the firstborn, the only child is likely to be achievement-
oriented. Both are over-represented in the upper I.Q. group
and number among select groups of students in colleges and
universities. According to Lucille Forer, however, there is a
difference between firstborn and only children:

The latter seem more motivated by a wish to
please someone who is important to them rather
than by any internalized self-requirements for such
achievement. They are more comfortable, than the
first child followed by siblings, if they do not achieve
at a high level. This more relaxed attitude probably
occurs because there is no sibling rival to force the
only child to make the parents' ambitions . . . his
own . . . in competing with the younger brother or
sister.[7]

Unlike the firstborn, the only child has never had to cope
with the trauma of "dethronement." He has no fear that a
younger sibling will replace him in his parents' affections; he

remains their sole heir, their pride and joy. His desire to please his parents motivates him to achieve; but anxiety, says Dr. Forer, is a much less prominent component of his motivation than it is for the firstborn. Whereas the firstborn's self-esteem depends on his achievement, the only child seems to accept his parents' pleasure in him as evidence that he is a person of worth.

Unfortunately, the same factors that produce high self-esteem often lead to self-centeredness. Since the lives of both parents usually revolve around the only child, he comes to believe that they live solely to serve him and his needs. It is not surprising that "onlies" of both sexes grow up feeling that all of life should revolve around them.

Individualism can have its advantages, as we shall see in the next chapter when we study the life of John the Baptist. But the wrong desire for special standing can be a real hindrance to Christian fellowship. Paul warns Christians to "do nothing from selfishness or conceit, but in humility count others better than yourselves" (Philippians 2:3). Any child accustomed to being on center-stage faces quite an adjustment when he must learn to fit into the Body of Christ.

To put it simply, the problem of the only child is just the opposite of that faced by most people when they become Christians. Most of us have grown up with low self-esteem, and it is hard for us to believe that we are special to God. The only child knows he is special; his problem is in realizing that *all* God's kids are special.

## The Only Child and His Friends

One disappointment for children from one-child families is that they often have difficulty forming close relationships with others. Siblings are very much aware of one another's faults and failures, and it comes as no shock to them that their friends have similar shortcomings. Only children, however, tend to harbor unrealistic expectations, as Murray Kappelman points out, seeking the qualities they desire in an idealized brother or sister, and thus dooming real-life relationships to failure.[8]

To make up for the lack of peers within the family, only children have been known to invent imaginary playmates—a topic of considerable interest to our group of only children. Sandy explained that one of her imaginary friends was good and another was bad. She played with the "good" friend when she was happy, and the "bad" friend when she was angry.

But imaginary playmates do not prepare a child for the real world of competition, jealousy and strife, and many single children never learn to handle relationships. Several in our group confessed that real-life friends, especially Christian friends, often disappointed them.

Because the only child has never had to compete with siblings for attention and has never had to share his toys and clothes with others in the family, there is as a rule little competitiveness and jealousy in his makeup. He finds it difficult, therefore, to accept these qualities in others, especially in those who call themselves Christians. If the only child is to develop lasting and satisfactory relationships, he will have to learn to be tolerant and understanding of the struggle that others have with these problems.

A child's parents, no matter how kind and loving, cannot make up for the interplay that takes place between brothers and sisters within a family, which will always remain a mystery to the only child. Imagine, then, how he must feel when he comes into a Christian community, where he has many sisters and brothers! Being thrust into large group situations can pose an emotional threat.

I witnessed such an internal upheaval in my four-year-old niece, Lisa, who once spent a week with our family while her mother was out-of-town. Lisa, at that time an only child, was accustomed to her parents' undivided attention. After a week of competing with my three oldest children—all very vocal—for her share of attention, Lisa developed a bad stutter. When my sister came home I told her to ignore the stuttering, which I was sure would disappear as soon as Lisa was once again the sole recipient of adult attention. Sure enough, she stopped stuttering within a few weeks and has never had a recurrence of the problem.

Perhaps Lisa's case provides an analogy of what happens to "onlies" within the family of God. Struggling to compete for attention in the bewildering world of brothers and sisters, it may take time to learn to communicate freely and participate fully in the give-and-take of family life.

Researchers, even those who staunchly defend the one-child family, agree that loneliness and protective isolation are major drawbacks for the only child. König assesses the single child by saying that he

> is a lonely child. He longs to be with others, but when he is, he wants to be alone. This is the ambiguous position of an only child's emotions: to meet and be one with others, and to refrain from doing so at the same time. . . . This ambivalence becomes so deeply ingrained that it remains with him for the rest of his life.[9]

Because of this, he adds, the only child finds it difficult to enter into the "fulness of life but stands at the threshold of existence."[10]

My report on these research findings brought a strong response from our group of only children. Bob was the first to speak: "I always felt I wanted to be part of something—but as soon as I put one foot in, I would think, *I'd rather be by myself.* I almost feel that the only person I can talk to is me. I'm the greatest thing going, and I don't need anyone else!"

Immediately Pat chimed in, "I wanted to mix with people, but then I would feel threatened and think it was more comfortable with just me. I expected people to be better than they were, and when they failed me I withdrew more and more."

Surprisingly, the group was in total agreement with König's assessment. When I asked, "Do you like to be alone?", Joe's reply was the perfect proof of the only child's ambivalent attitude: "I do and I don't," he said.

I pointed out to the group that this ambivalence of feelings could lead to indecisiveness and a lack of conviction, producing a lukewarm Christianity. My suggestion found support from Ron, who confessed that when he was in high school, even though he strongly disapproved of using alcohol, he often drank with his friends—because that's what "the gang" was doing.

This lack of conviction is a problem that the Christian "only" needs to deal with. Someone has said, "If we don't stand for anything, we will fall for everything," and the only child is in danger of doing just that. As we study Samson's life in the next chapter, we will see how his lack of conviction brought about his downfall.

## A Dwarf Among Giants

Dr. Murray Kappelman, the author of *Raising the Only Child,* stated that such children may exhibit either extreme independence or dependence. Both come from a deep-seated insecurity. "Extreme dependency," Dr. Kappelman believes, "usually results when parents treat their only child like a helpless creature. . . . " The manifestations of exaggerated independence, he says, include "the need to shun authority figures, to assume leadership, to dominate conversations and activities," all of which traits "stem from the strong need to control all aspects of a situation . . . a deep inner insecurity about what may result if control is lost."[11]

The only child has good reason to feel like "a helpless creature." He spends his entire childhood among adults whose abilities are naturally far superior to his. He is, as Rudolf Dreikurs has said, "a dwarf among giants"[12]; although, paradoxically, his behavior may seem mature, since he has been raised in the company of adults. Explains Dr. Forer,

> Thus he presents to other people, particularly those in relatively casual relationships, a usual image of being independent and capable. But inside the only child may feel quite different from the way other people see him. Having filled the role for many years of being a child with two adults, he continues to feel as a child.[13]

Like the youngest, he has never had any younger sibling on whom to test out his power. All his life, he may feel like a child while acting like a parent.

Joan, one of the women in our sample group, confided that she was having conflicts with her two oldest children. As her story unfolded, it was apparent that she was competing with her two children. Although on the surface she appeared to be a competent wife and mother, she still felt like a child herself. Many of her difficulties were resolved when Joan deliberately made an effort to see herself in each area of conflict as the mother rather than the child.

The firstborn child goes through life seeking relationships in which he can be parental; the last-born often desires to remain a child. The only child, being a combination of oldest and youngest, may mimic his parents by *acting* parental, while inside *feeling* like a child. Here again, the only child's ambivalence is manifested. Because he appears parental, he may attract friends who desire to be dominated and protected; but such friends cannot meet his need to be a child. Perhaps in part as a consequence of this ambivalence, many adults who grew up as only children have a string of broken relationships in their lives.

Though modern psychology would have us believe that the only child is the most deficient emotionally, bearing the deepest scars, we must remember one thing: that God is about the business of redeeming, reconciling all things to Himself and fashioning something good out of all that is imperfect in our lives. No one is locked into a past life, hopelessly doomed throughout his years to suffer from the scars of childhood. God Himself wants to take the weaknesses of the only child and fashion them into strengths for His own good purposes— as we shall see.

# Chapter 12

# The Receivers

Only children, especially those born to older parents, grow up as a rule with the knowledge that they are special. In many cases the mother has had difficulty in conceiving or carrying a child to term, and the birth of a live baby is looked upon almost as a miracle. No wonder such a child grows up feeling special!

Samson's birth was doubly miraculous. Not only did it end his mother's barrenness; his conception was foretold by *two* visits from the angel of the Lord (Judges 13), who made it clear that he was to be a Nazirite, dedicated to God from his birth. One thing was certain: Samson was a special child. It appears that his parents later had other children (16:31), but Samson probably spent his early years as an "only."

Perhaps the angel who instructed Samson's parents about his upbringing should have mentioned the importance of discipline, for they seem to have indulged him excessively. When we are first introduced to Samson in Judges 14, he is demanding that his parents get him a Philistine woman for his wife. When his father and mother demurred, his imperious answer was, "Get her for me; for she pleases me well" (v. 3). Like the typical only child described by Lucille Forer, Samson learned early that to get what he wanted, all he had to do was ask.

At his wedding feast, Samson told a riddle for the thirty Philistines who had been invited. He bet them sixty garments that they could not find the solution, and they accepted his wager. When the young men realized that they were about to lose the bet, they went to Samson's wife and threatened to kill her if she did not entice her husband to tell her the answer. It took seven days of weeping, but she finally broke down Samson's resistance and got the answer from him.

In the preceding chapter, I discussed the close relationship between the male single child and his mother, and the danger of his becoming a "mother's boy." Like Samson, such men are often manipulated by women all their lives.

His wife's deception enraged Samson so much that he killed thirty innocent Philistines from another town and gave their garments to those who had answered his riddle.

Inordinate anger is often a characteristic of the only child. Lucille Forer believes this is because he feels almost *too* secure:

> A child with brothers and sisters feels, con- sciously or unconsciously, that if he goes too far in aggravating the parents, they may "throw him out" and keep the others. The only child rarely feels this way. I believe that is why only children sometimes develop extreme anger. . . . [1]

Children who are used to being angry and demanding of their earthly parents are likely to approach their heavenly Father with this same attitude.

Samson's anger and his attraction to Philistine women got him into hot water more than once (see Judges 16:1-3), and eventually proved to be his undoing. When he fell in love with Delilah, the rulers of the Philistines bribed her to discover the secret of his superhuman strength. At first Samson met Deli- lah's wiles with his own brand of deceitfulness. When she pressed him day after day, however, "his soul was vexed to death" (v. 16) and he finally told her what she wanted to know.

The rest of the story is all too familiar. When Samson's long hair—the sign of his dedication to God—was shaved, the Lord left him and he became as weak as any normal man. The Philistines gouged out his eyes and set him to grinding grain in the prison.

One day, as the Philistines were making sport of him at a festival, God gave him strength once again and he pulled down the pillars of the house, slaying more men at his death than he had killed during his life. Even his last prayer, however, was totally self-centered: "Strengthen me, I pray thee, only this once, O God, that I may be avenged upon the Philistines for one of my two eyes" (verse 28). Like all his other feats of strength, Samson's final achievement was carried out, not for God's glory, but for his own gratification.

Samson is a stereotype of the indulged only child: self-centered, thinking only of his own pleasure and desires, and easily manipulated by women. It is paradoxical that God gave to a man of such weak character the greatest physical strength of any man who ever lived. Granted special standing and privilege from the womb, Samson ended his life in disgrace, still striking out in anger.

In Chapter 11, I quoted Alfred Adler as saying that only children often become "useless for life." Although God in His providence used Samson's weaknesses (as well as his physical strength) to end the Philistines' domination of Israel, Samson was worse than useless as a son and husband.

## The Blessings of Trust

In comparison to the other biblical characters we have studied—Abraham, who left home and family to follow God;

Jacob, who wrestled with God; Moses, who persuaded Pharoah to "let My people go"; Joseph and his sensational rise from slavery to a position of power in Egypt—Isaac seems pale and uninteresting. Theologians see Isaac as a type of Christ, the heir by divine promise (Galatians 4:23) who was laid by his father on the altar and received back as from the dead (Hebrews 11:19). The only child can learn tremendous practical lessons, however, from an examination of Isaac's character.

A distinctive aspect of Isaac's story is that he seemed to be a very passive person. Passivity is a frequent characteristic of the only child and, like many other character traits, it can be desirable, if not carried to an extreme.

The study reported in the May 1976 issue of *Psychology Today* suggested that only children, lacking the constant competition of other siblings, grow up trusting the motives of other people. And nowhere is the trusting nature of the only child demonstrated more clearly than in Isaac, who allowed Abraham to bind him on the altar of sacrifice (Genesis 22). Since Isaac was old enough to carry the wood, he was surely strong enough to overpower his aged father; yet he submitted without a struggle.

Isaac was equally trusting in the matter of his marriage. Once Abraham had decided that Isaac's wife should come from his own kindred, he sent his servant to Mesopotamia with orders to choose a woman from his brother's village to be Isaac's bride (Genesis 24). When the servant returned with Rebekah, Isaac received her as his wife.

There is an interesting scriptural comment that, in his love for Rebekah, "Isaac was comforted after his mother's death" (v. 67). Sarah died when Isaac was 37 (Genesis 17:17; 18:10; 23:1); and at the time of his marriage to Rebekah he was 40 (Genesis 25:20). At least three years had passed since his mother's death, yet Isaac was still mourning. Typical of the male single child, Isaac obviously had a strong attachment to his mother.

Scripture tells us that, even though Abraham had numerous other sons by his second wife, Keturah, yet he "gave all he had to Isaac" (Genesis 25:5). God was equally generous to him. When Isaac sowed, the Lord blessed him and he "reaped in the same year a hundredfold . . . and . . . became very wealthy" (Genesis 26:12-13). God blessed him, not for what he had done, but for what his father had done: "because Abraham obeyed my voice and kept my charge, my commandments, my statutes, and my laws" (v. 5). In short, Isaac never had to work very hard for what he possessed.

Like Isaac, most single children are used to receiving, especially from their parents. As a result, they may become both passive and dependent, especially the female only child, who may seek the care and attention of older persons willing to assume a quasi-parental role.

In marriage, the only child is likely to remain the more passive partner. Isaac never represented much of an authority figure; and, like Samson, he allowed himself to be manipulated by his wife, whose bold and successful plot tricked Isaac into giving their second-born son, Jacob, the blessing that belonged to his older twin, Esau. In general, the tendency of male single children to marry domineering wives may develop if they are looking for marriage partners who will give them the undivided attention, esteem and care that were provided by their mothers.

The dependency of female only children is probably responsible, to a large degree, for the low divorce rate among such women. Research suggests that they are reluctant to share their spouses with anyone, and will often stand by the most unsuitable spouse in the interests of security.[2]

When a famine came to Canaan, Isaac went to Gerar in the land of the Philistines (Genesis 26). Gerar is halfway between Canaan, the Promised Land, and Egypt, representing the world. Whereas Abraham went all the way to Egypt in a time of famine, his son remained between the world and the Promised Land—an appropriate position for the only child with his ambivalent nature.

Likewise, this ambivalence causes many single children to become "middle-of-the-road" Christians, satisfied to remain in Gerar rather than make the effort to come all the way into the Promised Land.

Although Isaac was one of the patriarchs of Israel and lived to be 180, his story is contained in a few brief chapters of Genesis. After we are told how he was deceived by Rebekah and Jacob, we hear nothing more about him until eight chapters later, when we read that "Isaac breathed his last" (Genesis 35:28).

In Watchman Nee's book *Changed into His Likeness*, the life of Isaac is summed up as follows:

> This fact of bestowal and acceptance is the great great characteristic of Isaac. The God of Isaac is God the Giver. . . . As the God of Isaac he comes to us and gives us everything in his Son.[3]

Isaac and Samson had this characteristic in common: God continually blessed them, and all they did was *receive*. The best thing that born-again onlies have going for them is this ability to receive. Used to receiving from parents, the only child has little trouble receiving from God, or accepting every blessing that is offered.

The first time I ever shared the message of salvation, it was with a friend who is an only child. When I told her what God had done in my life, she was so responsive that I could hardly believe it. Her response was, "That's great! I want it, too." And from that time on, she was a born-again Christian. My own entrance into the Kingdom came after so much searching and wrestling with God that I was at a loss to understand how her new birth could be so effortless!

In our area there is a minister who is an only child. He teaches the doctrine of grace almost exclusively, telling over and over again what Christ has done for us, and emphasizing the fact that our only responsibility is to receive. This aspect of the gospel is the one that he, as an only child, understands best.

God is not only the God of Isaac, however; He is also the God of Jacob. These two experiences run parallel throughout Scripture. Watchman Nee pointed out that

> Isaac . . . speaks to us of God's impartation to us of Christ, whereas Jacob illustrates our disciplinary schooling by the Holy Spirit. Isaac reminds us of God's gifts made over to us absolutely, a reminder that gives us wonderful confidence and assurance. Jacob, on the other hand, draws our attention to the Spirit's inward working upon us to form Christ within, a working whose costliness draws forth rather our fear and trembling. . . . Jacob causes us to know our own extreme weakness and uselessness. In Isaac we boldly proclaim that sin is beneath our feet; yet in Jacob we tremblingly confess that as long as we live we may fall again. These two together, Isaac with his confidence in Christ, and Jacob with his self-knowledge, are the life of the Christian.[4]

A dilemma common among born-again only children was

described by Ron: "I can really receive from God, but when it comes to walking it out—that's when I have trouble." The greatest spiritual strength of the single child is his ability to receive. Yet the greatest hurdle to overcome is a reluctance to press on—to "run with perseverance the race" (Hebrews 12:1).

The majority of born-again only children seem to stay in the Isaac category. They are able to receive from God, but never learn to press on to become dynamic Christians. Yet it was an only child, John the Baptist, who was described by our Lord as the greatest "among those born of women" (Matthew 11:11). What was it that caused John to leave the safety of the middle to become the herald of God's Kingdom on earth?

John entered the world in much the same way as Samson. Both mothers had suffered the disgrace of barrenness; both births were foretold by an angel; both children were to be Nazirites and were filled with the Holy Spirit from the womb. Yet their lives, which had almost identical beginnings, ended so differently: Samson's in a vengeful suicide; John's in selfless martyrdom.

We know nothing about the childhood of John the Baptist, but Luke tells us that "he was *in the wilderness* till the day of his manifestation to Israel" (Luke 1:80; italics added). It appears that John grew up a very solitary child—what today we would call a "loner." He had no siblings to keep him company, and we can imagine that his aged parents provided very little companionship. Having become used to solitude as a small child, he doubtless found it natural to spend long hours alone in the wilderness. Again we see how God designs our birth order to develop those characteristics that will be most beneficial to the ministry He has planned for us.

Among the astronauts who had traveled into space by the end of 1968, according to a report in *Newsweek* (January 6, 1969), was a proportion of only children far greater than what could be expected from the general population. The corresponding explanation suggested that only children may develop greater independence, self-reliance and courage since they spend more of their childhoods alone.

Independence and courage are certainly attributes of John the Baptist, who was intimidated by neither religious leaders nor kings. But John, instead of becoming self-reliant during his time alone, became God-reliant—and that makes a world of difference.

I explained in the last chapter that only children, like the youngest in the family, may be either overly dependent or extremely independent. The dependence we saw in Samson and Isaac makes a marked contrast with John's independent individualism. He seems to fit Lucille Forer's description of the single child who has

> strong and intense attitudes and feelings and usually is quite an individualistic person in adulthood. He is likely to draw the attention of other people and often their admiration because he seems to feel so comfortable being the special kind of person he is likely to feel himself to be.[5]

Like Samson and Isaac, John was a child of promise and *knew* he was special. Receiving the prophetic utterances made about him, and the gift of the Holy Spirit that was his from birth, John withdrew from the world in order to spend time alone with God and prepare himself to fulfill those prophecies:

> And he will turn many of the sons of Israel to the Lord their God, and he will go before him in the spirit and power of Elijah. . . .
>
> (Luke 1:16-17)

Both Samson and Isaac were dependent on their parents and on the women in their lives; but John had transferred his dependence to God. Because he was totally dependent on God, he was totally independent of people and their approval.

To most Christians today it may seem that John went too far in his individualism and lack of concern for public opinion. He was a nonconformist both in clothing—wearing "a garment of camel's hair, and a leather girdle around his waist"—and in his diet—"locusts and wild honey" (Matthew 3:4).

But our group of only children was deeply impressed by John's forceful, dynamic nature: "He didn't have that ambivalent nature of the only child," they said. "He was decisive, with strong commitments. He wasn't doubleminded, but stable. There were no gray areas about him; he exposed sin and didn't care what people thought."

Our group of "Isaacs" found inspiration and encouragement in the story of John, who feared God rather than men and who was decisive rather than passive or ambivalent, singleminded rather than doubleminded. I could almost read their thoughts: *John was an only child, and he made it. It is possible for me, too.*

# Chapter 13

# A Final Word

Just as I brought the last dish into the dining room, I overheard a snatch of conversation that almost caused me to drop my favorite broccoli-cheese casserole on the floor.

"I just *knew* you were a firstborn the moment we were introduced," June was saying to one of our houseguests from England. "I'm a firstborn myself and can always spot another one." In her best clinical voice, June proceeded to expound on the firstborn characteristics that our dinner guest displayed.

After the casserole was safely deposited on the table, I hurried back into the kitchen to compose myself. What had I done to the members of our sample groups? Ever since June had attended the meeting of firstborns from our fellowship, she had been fascinated with the effects of birth order and had read all she could find on the subject. Lately she had started displaying her knowledge by analyzing everyone she met.

After dinner, when June and most of the other guests had left, I apologized to Michael, the visiting minister whom she had analyzed.

"It's quite understandable," he replied. "We need psychologically oriented books that are written from a Christian perspective. But some people who read a book like yours come to consider themselves authorities in the field, and become amateur analysts. Someone like June could end up losing a lot of friends and alienating a great many people if she goes around giving lectures on birth order to everyone she meets."

Michael's warning hit home. It is much easier, I have learned, to be objective about a friend's weaknesses than about my own. Something in me resists facing *myself* as I really am. I might be willing to let God "search me . . . and know my heart. . . . And see if there be any wicked way in me" (Psalm 139:23-24), but I would rather that He reveal His findings in me privately, if at all.

Because it is painful to let God show us who we really are, many Christians remain unchanged after salvation. Yet it is only when we know the truth about ourselves that the truth can make us free (see John 8:32).

The most important purpose of this book is to help each of us understand ourselves a little better. Some people consciously or subconsciously resist identifying with others in the same birth order because of an understandable reluctance to be labeled. Each of us can readily identify, for example, with characteristics of birth orders different from our own. It is also true that no two people have identical experiences or personalities, and that each of us is unique.

But most of us, in order to cope with the world we live in, develop a mask made up of characteristics that hide rather than reflect our true natures. The person I *really* am may be buried under so many layers of insulation that God will have to peel me like an onion in order to reveal to me my basic nature. Adam and Eve began the cover-up with fig leaves, and the human race has continued to add more and more layers to hide our spirits as well as our bodies.

In the seventh chapter of Romans, Paul describes the conflict he experienced when he came face-to-face with his true inner nature. Having faced himself honestly—perhaps for the first time since his conversion many years earlier—Paul was finally able to cry exultantly, "There is therefore now no condemnation for those who are in Christ Jesus. For the law of the Spirit of life in Christ Jesus has set me free from the law of sin and death" (Romans 8:1-2).

Until we recognize where we are in bondage, God cannot set us free. And until we ourselves have been set free, He cannot use us to bring other people into freedom. Only those people who truly know themselves are equipped to help others gain self-understanding. Before I attempt to remove that speck from my brother's eye, I had better let God remove the log that is in my own (see Matthew 7:3-5).

Each of us is in danger when we simply tolerate in ourselves the peculiarities associated with our position in the family. Behavior that is contrary to the Word of God may be understandable, but it is never acceptable. Once we understand the weaknesses to which our own birth order makes us susceptible, we must open them to God, who will transform them into His strength.

I myself recognized recently that my trouble in overcoming certain sins in my life was due in part to the fact that I had never called them by their real names. I had always considered myself "persuasive" rather than manipulative; "sensitive" rather than rebellious; "agreeable" rather than repressive—and the list of euphemisms went on and on.

I experienced a tremendous freedom in being able to confess to God that I was a manipulator, a rebel, and that I repressed my true emotions. Calling my sins by their true names, with no excuses or euphemisms to confuse the issue, brought that freedom. And now, at last, I feel that God is helping me to turn these negative qualities into their positive counterparts. One of the greatest promises we have as Christians is that God's "strength is made perfect in weakness" (II Corinthians 12:9, KJV).

The research I have done for this book has given me a much greater appreciation of the Church as the Body of Christ, and a deeper understanding of Paul's description of the Body in I Corinthians 12:14-31. The differing gifts and ministries described in this passage are obvious.

Now, however, it seems to me that Paul also had in mind the differing character traits given to each member of the Body. Imagine a man with the faith of Abraham, the persistence of Jacob, the humility of Moses, the enthusiasm and love of David, and the courage of John the Baptist. Such a "man" still exists as the Body of Christ with Jesus as our Head. Only as we function together—each of us recognizing his need for every other member—will the Church fulfill its mission of making the Kingdom of heaven a reality on earth.

# Index

**Chapter 1, Relating in God's Family**

1. Alfred Adler, *What Life Should Mean To You* (New York: Capricorn Books, G. P. Putnam's Sons, 1958), pp. 154-155.
2. Karl König, *Brothers and Sisters* (Blauvelt, New York: St. George Books, 1963), p. 21.
3. Elizabeth Hurlock, *Child Development* (New York: McGraw-Hill Book Co., 1972), p. 445.
4. Lucille K. Forer, *Birth Order and Life Roles* (Springfield, Ill.: Charles C. Thomas, Pub., 1969), p. 140.

**Chapter 2, The Family "Constellation"**

1. Lucille K. Forer, *Birth Order and Life Roles* (Springfield, Ill.: Charles C. Thomas, Pub., 1969), p. 15.
2. Lucille K. Forer, *The Birth Order Factor* (New York: David McKay Co., Inc., 1976), p. 17.
3. Walter Toman, *Family Constellation* (New York: Springer Publishing Co., 1961), p. 17.
4. Lucille K. Forer, *The Birth Order Factor*, p. 27.
5. Karl König, *Brothers and Sisters* (Blauvelt, New York: St. George Books, 1963), p. 15.
6. James H. S. Bossard, *The Large Family System* (Philadelphia: University of Pennsylvania Press, 1956), p. 220.
7. Lucille K. Forer, *Birth Order and Life Roles*, p. 109.
8. Lucille K. Forer, *The Birth Order Factor*, p. 36.
9. Philip S. Very and Nancy P. Van Hine, "Effects of Birth Order upon Personality Development of Twins," *The Journal of Genetic Psychology*, V. 114 (1969), pp. 93-95.

## Chapter 3, The Firstborn

1. Edith G. Neisser, *The Eldest Child* (New York: Harper & Bros., 1957), p. 72.
2. Neisser, p. 3.
3. Karl König, *Brothers and Sisters* (Blauvelt, New York: St. George Books, 1963), p. 36.
4. *International Bible Dictionary* (Plainfield, N.J.: Logos International, 1977), p. 65.
5. Lucille K. Forer, *Birth Order and Life Roles* (Springfield, Ill.: Charles C. Thomas, Pub., 1969), p. 39.
6. König, p. 40.
7. Forer, p. 102.
8. Forer, p. 94.
9. Alfred Adler, *What Life Should Mean to You* (New York: Capricorn Books, G. P. Putnam's Sons, 1958), p. 146.
10. Forer, p. 98.
11. Forer, p. 57.
12. Walter Toman, *Family Constellation* (New York: Springer Publishing Co., Third Edition, 1976), p. 153.
13. Forer, p. 62.
14. James H. S. Bossard, *The Large Family System* (Philadelphia: University of Pennsylvania Press, 1956), pp. 158-159.

## Chapter 4, Free to Be Me

1. Karl König, *Brothers and Sisters* (Blauvelt, New York: St. George Books, 1963), pp. 56-57.
2. Edith G. Neisser, *The Eldest Child* (New York: Harper & Bros., 1957), p. 45.
3. Heinz L. Ansbacher and Rowena R. Ansbacher, *The Individual Psychology of Alfred Adler* (New York: Harper & Row, 1964), pp. 378-379.

**Chapter 5, The Second-Born**

1. Charles McArthur, "Personalities of First and Second Children," *Psychiatry,* 19, (1956), pp. 47-54.
2. Alfred Fischer, "Psychologic Aspects of Pediatrics," *J. of Pediatrics,* 40, (1952), pp. 254-259.
3. Joan Lasko, "Parent Behavior Toward First and Second Children," *Genetic Psychology Monographs,* 49, (1954), pp. 96-137.
4. Virginia Crandall, Walter Katkovsky and Vaughn Crandall, "Children's Beliefs in Their Own Control of Reinforcements in Intellectual-Academic Achievement Situations," *Child Development,* pp. 105-106.
5. Lucille Forer, *The Birth Order Factor* (New York: David McKay Co., Inc., 1976), p. 53.
6. Lucille Forer, p. 54.
7. Walter Toman, *Family Constellation* (New York: Springer Publishing Co., 1976), p. 17.
8. Forer, p. 58.
9. Charles McArthur, pp. 47-54.
10. Heinz L. Ansbacher and Rowena R. Ansbacher, *The Individual Psychology of Alfred Adler* (New York: Harper & Row, 1964), quoted by Lucille Forer, *Birth Order and Life Roles* (Springfield, Ill.: Charles C. Thomas, Pub., 1969), p. 51.
11. Alfred Adler, *What Life Should Mean to You* (New York: Capricorn Books, G. P. Putnam's Sons, 1958), p. 149.

**Chapter 6, The Dreamers and the Racers**

1. Karl König, *Brothers and Sisters* (Blauvelt, New York: St. George Books, 1963), pp. 57-58.
2. James Bossard, *The Large Family System* (Philadelphia: University of Pennsylvania Press, 1956), p. 220.
3. Alfred Adler, quoted by König, p. 54.

## Chapter 7, The Third-Born

1. Karl König, *Brothers and Sisters* (Blauvelt, New York: St. George Books, 1963), p. 76.
2. König, p. 77.

## Chapter 8, The Power of Meekness

1. William Barclay, *The Beatitudes and The Lord's Prayer for Everyman* (New York: Harper & Row, Publishers, 1975), pp. 38-39, 46.
2. Karl König, *Brothers and Sisters* (Blauvelt, New York: St. George Books, 1963), p. 80.
3. Barclay, p. 46.

## Chapter 9, The Last-Born

1. Brian Sutton-Smith, B. G. Rosenberg, *The Sibling* (New York: Holt, Rinehart and Winston, Inc., 1970), p. 154.
2. Rudolf Dreikurs, *The Challenge of Parenthood* (New York: Hawthorn Books, Inc., 1958), p. 47.
3. Alfred Adler, *Understanding Human Nature* (New York: Fawcett World Library, 1969), p. 123.
4. Adler, pp. 124-125.
5. Lucille Forer, *Birth Order and Life Roles* (Springfield, Ill.: Charles C. Thomas, Pub., 1969), p. 124.
6. Georgia Babladelis, "Birth Order and Responsiveness to Social Influence," *Psychological Reports,* 30 (1), (Feb. 1972), pp. 99-104.
7. Lucille Forer, *The Birth Order Factor* (New York: David McKay Co., Inc., 1976), p. 136.
8. Ross Stagner and E. T. Katzoff, "Personality as Related to Birth Order and Family Size," *Journal of Applied Psychology,* 20, (1936), pp. 340-346
9. Alfred Adler, *What Life Should Mean To You* (New York: Capricorn Books, G. P. Putnam's Sons, 1958), p. 151.
10. Adler, *What Life Should Mean To You,* p. 128.
11. Forer, *The Birth Order Factor,* p. 12.

12. Norman Miller and Geoffrey Maruyama, "Ordinal Position and Peer Popularity," *J. Pers. Soc. Psychol.*, 33, (Feb. 1976), pp. 123-131.

**Chapter 10, The Last Who Will Be First**

1. Walter Toman, *Family Constellation* (New York: Springer Publishing Co., 1976, Third Edition), p. 157.
2. Toman, p. 157.

**Chapter 11, The Only Child**

1. Alfred Adler, *Understanding Human Nature* (New York: Fawcett World Library, 1969), p. 127.
2. Bruce Cushna, Mitchell Greene & Bill C. F. Snider, "First Born and Last Born Children in a Child Development Clinic," *J. Individ. Psychol*, 20, (1964), pp. 179-182, quoted by Lucille Forer in *Birth Order and Life Roles* (Springfield, Ill.: Charles C. Thomas, Pub., 1969), p. 67.
3. Heinz Ansbacher & Rowena Ansbacher, *The Individual Psychology of Alfred Adler* (New York: Harper & Row, 1956), p. 381.
4. Norma E. Cutts & Nicholas Mosely, *The Only Child* (New York: G. P. Putnam's Sons, 1954), p. 36.
5. Murray Kappelman, *Raising the Only Child* (New York: The New American Library, Inc., 1975), p. 13.
6. Lucille Forer, *The Birth Order Factor* (New York: David McKay Co., Inc., 1976), p. 162.
7. Forer, *Birth Order and Life Roles*, p. 70.
8. Kappelman, p. 51.
9. Karl König, *Brothers and Sisters* (Blauvelt, N.Y.: St. George Books, 1963), pp. 28, 30.
10. König, p. 30.
11. Kappelman, p. 33.
12. Rudolf Dreikurs, *The Challenge of Parenthood* (New York: Hawthorn Books, Inc., 1958), p. 47.

13. Forer, *Birth Order and Life Roles*, p. 83.

## Chapter 12, The Receivers

1. Lucille Forer, *The Birth Order Factor* (New York: David McKay Company, Inc., 1976), p. 270.
2. Lucille Forer, *Birth Order and Life Roles* (Springfield, Ill.: Charles C. Thomas, Pub., 1969), p. 91.
3. Watchman Nee, *Changed into His Likeness* (Wheaton, Ill.: Tyndale House Publishers, 1978), p. 100.
4. Nee, pp. 119-120.
5. Forer, *Birth Order and Life Roles*, p. 71.

# Bibliography

Alfred Adler, *Understanding Human Nature.* New York: Fawcett World Library, 1969.

Alfred Adler, *What Life Should Mean to You.* New York: Capricorn Books, G. P. Putnam's Sons, 1958.

Heinz L. Ansbacher & Rowena R. Ansbacher, *The Individual Psychology of Alfred Adler.* New York: Harper & Row, 1964.

Georgia Babladelis, "Birth Order and Responsiveness to Social Influence." *Psychological Reports,* 30 (1), February 1972.

William Barclay, *The Beatitudes and the Lord's Prayer for Everyman.* New York: Harper & Row, 1975.

James H. S. Bossard, *The Large Family System.* Philadelphia: University of Pennsylvania Press, 1956.

Virginia Crandall, Walter Katkovsky & Vaughn Crandall, "Children's Beliefs in their Own Control of Reinforcements in Intellectual-Academic Achievement Situations." *Child Development.*

Bruce Cushna, Mitchell Greene & Bill C. F. Snider, "First Born and Last Born Children in a Child Development Clinic," *J. Indiv. Psychol.,* 20, 1964, quoted by Lucille Forer in *Birth Order and Life Roles* (see below).

Norma E. Cutts & Nicholas Mosely, *The Only Child.* New York: G. P. Putnam's Sons, 1954.

Rudolf Dreikurs, *The Challenge of Parenthood.* New York: Hawthorn Books, Inc., 1958.

Alfred Fischer, "Psychologic Aspects of Pediatrics." *J. of Pediatrics,* 40, 1952.

Lucille K. Forer, *Birth Order and Life Roles.* Springfield, Ill.: Charles C. Thomas, Pub., 1969.

Lucille K. Forer, *The Birth Order Factor.* New York: David McKay Co., Inc., 1976.

Elizabeth Hurlock, *Child Development.* New York: McGraw-Hill Book Co., 1972.

*International Bible Dictionary.* Plainfield, N.J.: Logos International, 1977.

Murray Kappelman, *Raising the Only Child.* New York: The New American Library, Inc., 1975.

Karl König, *Brothers and Sisters.* Blauvelt, N.Y.: St. George Books, 1963.

Joan Lasko, "Parent Behavior Toward First and Second Children." *Genetic Psychology Monographs,* 49, 1954.

Charles McArthur, "Personalities of First and Second Children." *Psychiatry,* 19, 1956.

Norman Miller & Geoffrey Maruyama, "Ordinal Position and Peer Popularity." *J. Pers. Soc. Psychol.,* 33, February 1976.

Watchman Nee, *Changed into His Likeness.* Wheaton, Ill.: Tyndale House Publishers, 1978.

Edith G. Neisser, *The Eldest Child.* New York: Harper & Bros., 1957.

Ross Stagner & E. T. Katzoff, "Personality as Related to Birth Order and Family Size." *Journal of Applied Psychology,* 20, 1936.

Brian Sutton-Smith & B. G. Rosenberg, *The Sibling.* New York: Holt, Rinehart and Winston, Inc., 1970.

Walter Toman, *Family Constellation.* New York: Springer Publishing Co., 1961, and Third Edition, 1976.

Philip S. Very & Nancy P. Van Hine, "Effects of Birth Order upon Personality Development of Twins." *The Journal of Genetic Psychology,* V. 114, 1969.